I'M NOT ONE TO GOSSIP, BUT...

I'M NOT ONE TO GOSSIP, BUT...

Wicked Whispers, William
Hickey and Forty Years
of Blarney

JOHN McENTEE

Biteback Publishing

First published in Great Britain in 2016 by
Biteback Publishing Ltd
Westminster Tower
3 Albert Embankment
London SE1 7SP
Copyright © John McEntee 2016

ISBN 978-1-78590-094-5

10 9 8 7 6 5 4 3 2 1

A CIP catalogue record for this book is available from the British Library.

Set in Sabon by Adrian McLaughlin

Printed and bound in Great Britain by
CPI Group (UK) Ltd, Croydon CR0 4YY

MIX
Paper from
responsible sources
FSC
www.fsc.org   FSC® C020471

To my children, Laura, Paul and Jack

CONTENTS

PREFACE

Caroline Aherne was possessed of many demons. One of them was a weakness for the drink. Attractive, gloriously creative, the writer and star of TV's *The Royle Family* was very drunk when we first met in an upstairs bar of Soho's Groucho Club.

It was just after midnight and Caroline and her *Royle Family* co-star Craig Cash were relaxing after a long day filming at Television Centre on the South Bank.

Craig was seated at the piano, thumping out a honky-tonk version of the Roman Catholic hymn 'Faith of Our Fathers'. Caroline, hair dishevelled, blouse open, displaying a little too much of her impressive cleavage, was unsteadily upright alongside the piano, clutching a large vodka and cranberry juice and warbling the words of the hymn. Seated next to Craig was the Welsh-born TV journalist Jaci Stephen, a friend of mine.

It was the summer of 1999 and I had just finished supper in a second-floor dining room at the Groucho with my then-editor Rosie Boycott and other department heads at the *Daily Express*. At the time I was the paper's William Hickey gossip columnist.

Rosie had little interest in the diary. I was struggling to tempt celebrities to a series of National Treasure lunches I had devised to raise the profile of Hickey and attract fashionable names to the *Express*. This was before the term 'National Treasure' became a cliché, and the lunches were held in the *Express* top-floor boardroom in Ludgate House, alongside Blackfriars Bridge. A date had been fixed for the next one the following week. But I was devoid of star names to attend and impress Ms Boycott.

Trudging down the stairs with a proof copy of the following day's Hickey page sticking out of my jacket pocket, Jaci spotted me. 'Come and join us!' she shouted above the din of piano and hymn. Caroline and Craig continued belting out 'Faith of Our Fathers' as they nodded in my direction.

'Would you like a drink?' I asked as the hymn finally reached an end. Caroline thrust out her empty glass. 'Vodka and cranberry juice,' she declared with a smile.

As I stepped up to the bar to order the round, a previously unseen group of about ten men and women who had been sitting around the piano in the ill-lit gloom rose from their seats clutching empty glasses. It was the cast of the TV soap *Emmerdale*. They were clearly thirsty.

I felt obliged to repeat, mantra-like, the orders being barked from behind. 'Two vodka and tonics, three Becks, two gin and tonics.' I passed the parade of brimming glasses from the bar to the nearby glass-topped table.

Eventually all the drinks were ordered and the bill, to my consternation, came to over £90. I paid with a credit card. Transaction complete, I turned around to be engulfed in a vice-like embrace by Caroline.

Grateful for her refill, she slurred, 'You're a nice man.' She then toppled back and crashed bum-first onto the glass table, followed in the blink of an eye by yours truly. Glasses, chunks of ice, gin, vodka, bottles of tonic, cranberry juice, coke as well as wedges of lemon scattered across the table top and cascaded to the carpeted floor.

Miraculously, the table didn't shatter. We remained locked in a grotesque embrace atop the rubble of the round. Caroline rolled from under me and picked herself up, apparently undamaged.

As the barman busied himself mopping up the carnage, the cast of *Emmerdale* silently and speedily evaporated, leaving myself, Caroline, Craig and Jaci. I ordered replacement drinks.

The sing-song resumed. I enjoyed a merry couple of hours with Jaci and my two new celebrity friends. All went well until Caroline spotted the newspaper proof sticking out of the side pocket of my suit.

'What's this?' she asked as she whipped the proof from my pocket. Blearily, she blinked at the page. Her face dissolved into a grimace. Her eyes narrowed and she snarled, 'You're a fucking gossip columnist. You didn't tell me you were a fucking gossip columnist.'

I didn't reply as I was busy doing my impression of a Lough Erne pike just after it's been hooked and before its head gets battered on the floor of the boat.

She then leaped to her feet and began tearing the proof page into tiny squares, which she sprinkled on my head like snowflakes. When she finished, I rose and, with what I foolishly thought was a modicum of dignity, walked to the door, down the stairs and out into Dean Street.

It was an occupational hazard, I mused.

*   *   *

By the time I was confettied by Caroline I should have been immune to such slights. I'd been at the journalistic coalface for nearly thirty years, first as a junior reporter on my local newspaper, *The Anglo-Celt*, graduating to the newsroom of the Dublin *Irish Press* before arriving in the British capital as London correspondent of the Irish Press Group in 1975. After that, it was all downhill. I became a gossip columnist on the Londoner's Diary on the *Evening Standard*. My career as a serious journalist was over. No more bombing campaigns, murders, profound interviews with the likes of Norman Mailer, William Manchester and Anthony Burgess.

Instead, it morphed into a blur of literary parties, West End first nights, celebrity memorial services and frequent calls to the hapless Andrew Cavendish, Duke of Devonshire. He had foolishly founded the Polite Society and felt obliged to come to the telephone each time a reporter from the Londoner's Diary called to say hello. And all of this cocooned in the comfort blanket of the *Standard*'s generous expenses. After leaving the paper for *The Times*, I encountered former colleague Richard Littlejohn in the blackness of 'the plant', which housed *The Times* and *The Sun* in Fortress Wapping. Over hard drinks in Davy's Wine Bar by Tower Bridge, Richard raised his glass. 'A toast,' he bellowed, 'to the *Evening Standard*. Fleet Street's last luxury liner.'

After stints at the *Standard*, *The Times* and the *Sunday Express*, I fetched up as diarist Ross Benson's deputy on the *Daily Express*. Early in 1994, I had accepted an offer of a job from Ross. I had signed a contract and was about to tell *Sunday Express* editor Eve Pollard, Lady Lloyd, when I got a call from her husband, *Daily Express* editor Nick Lloyd. 'I feel a complete cunt, John, but you can't come down.' He explained that Eve had insisted that she would let me join the *Express* on the third floor below only if Nick relinquished his news editor Jon Craig to come and work on the *Sunday*. No swap, no job.

Determined to escape, I extracted from Eve's secretary a list of the cocktail parties, book launches and openings she had accepted invitations to in forthcoming weeks.

Whenever she turned up she found her loyal employee McEntee warbling, very badly, a version of Engelbert Humperdinck's hit 'Please Release Me'. She eventually relented and let me go.

It was a happy time and Ross was a joy to work with (though a better war correspondent than gossip columnist). During my first week I made the mistake of answering a telephone call from Ross's wife Ingrid Seward. Ross, an Olympic-class womaniser, was not at his desk. 'He is having his hair cut,' I explained. 'But he had his hair cut on Tuesday,' Mrs Benson snapped.

Loyal diary secretary Jeanette Bishop explained that Ross was with one of his numerous girlfriends and the haircut excuse was the wrong answer.

Poor Ross. Only fifty-six when he died suddenly after watching his beloved Chelsea beat Barcelona at home in the Champions League in 2005. Just before he left the *Express* in 1997 for the *Mail*, my colleague Chris Williams asked me to join him for a farewell supper for Ross and his wife Ingrid at the Ivy. Both chuckled about the current antics of Diana, Princess of Wales – Ingrid was editor of *Majesty* magazine and Ross quipped, 'Each night Mrs Benson and I get down on our knees at bedtime and thank God for the madness of the Princess of Wales.'

Three days later, Diana was dead after a car crash in a Paris tunnel. Ross, virtually hounded out of the *Express* by editor Richard Addis, had the gratification of returning as a freelance to write, at £1 a word, a Niagara of material, wedged between her demise and burial, for the paper that no longer wanted him.

His grief-stricken widow Ingrid found consolation of sorts with Sir Dai Llewellyn, a glorious chancer known as the Seducer of the Valleys. He was keen to make Ingrid Lady Llewellyn but she declined even after he was stricken with the cancer that would kill him. Losing two husbands in a short space of time would have been too much. Dai was a rotund figure, rendered svelte in his final year by the ravages of illness. He easily fitted into

Ross Benson's magnificent, hand-tailored wardrobe and did so with enthusiasm. Weeks before the end, I arranged a £1,000 fee for Dai to be photographed for the *Daily Mail*, staging a final reconciliation with his estranged brother Roddy, former squeeze of Princess Margaret. He posed alongside Roddy wearing Ross's blue blazer, cavalry twill trousers and bespoke shoes. I hope Ross had a celestial laugh.

By the millennium I was happily embedded as Rosie Boycott's diarist, with my by-lined column and £100,000 a year.

I often woke up blinking in the middle of the night in a cold sweat, thinking the champagne-fuelled carousel had finally stopped. I'd been found out, exposed as a charlatan and fired. Not quite yet. By then my marriage had ended, entirely through my own fault in a blur of expenses, drink and sex. Only my robust Irish peasant constitution prevented a physical implosion. Mercifully, I was never afflicted with the genuinely horrendous curse of depression.

My afternoons and nights were spent in Soho and elsewhere. My brilliant and loyal colleagues Kathryn Spencer, Julie Carpenter and Kate Bogandovich protected me like a trio of clucking hens. So much so that when I was eventually leaving the *Express* for the *Mail*, they presented me with a pocket A–Z in which Blackfriars Bridge, next to the *Express* building, was marked out in red and emblazoned with the caption: 'I'm on the Bridge.'

How many times those long-suffering diarists had to cope with my telephoned or texted mantra from Gerry's Club and elsewhere: 'I'm on the Bridge.' It should be on my gravestone.

Something had to give and Lord Hollick's sale of the *Express* to Richard Desmond, owner of such august titles as *Asian Babes*, was the catalyst. After the arrival of the cigar-chomping new proprietor on the newsroom floor, editor Rosie Boycott searched in vain for her star diarist to introduce him to Desmond.

I was nowhere to be found. 'I'm on the Bridge.'

Even before Desmond's arrival, I had been enjoying a series of jolly lunches with Robin Esser, managing editor at the *Daily Mail* and a close confidante of editor-in-chief Paul Dacre. The possibility of moving to the *Mail* was mooted over Chablis and oysters. Eventually I met Paul for breakfast at his palatial town house in Belgravia. A job offer was made. I agreed in secret to jump ship for a yet-to-be-defined role.

Desmond had started the brutal cost-cutting that was to reduce the *Express* to comic-book status. As I had been at the *Express* for ten years, I had ambitions to secure a substantial redundancy payment, particularly as the £40,000 Hollick had given me when he sold the paper had gone directly to my soon-to-be ex-wife.

I claimed to Desmond's Rasputin-like representative on earth that I was 'all diaried out' and wanted a change. But a leak to the *Daily Telegraph* media column The Minx about my departure to the *Mail* scuppered that windfall. Chris Williams wanted me to stay and became unfriendly when he believed I was going.

By then the column carried my name emblazoned across the top of the page. With months to go before any eventual departure, Chris called me into his office. 'I am changing the name of the column to The Insiders. Do you mind?' I replied, 'You can call it Bob the Fucking Builder for all I care,' and walked out of his office.

I joined the *Mail* and sat for three months doing nothing. I realised that Paul's strategy was to remove me from the *Express*. He clearly had no idea what to do with me when I finally berthed in Northcliffe House in Kensington.

I quickly discovered one thing. Everyone had been well disposed to me while I worked for the *Daily Express* for the simple reason that no one read the paper. It wasn't relevant (circulation is now below 500,000). The *Mail*, however, was the powerhouse of Fleet Street. Everyone had a view on the *Mail*. At functions, celebrities, politicians and the great and the good were venomous about the *Mail*. But one thing was clear: they all read the paper. It couldn't be ignored.

Eventually Paul devised a new gossip column for me. He had been an admirer of the US commentator Walter Winchell, who had a syndicated column called Wicked Whispers. Paul borrowed the title and I became editor of the *Mail*'s Wicked Whispers. It ran for four days a week – Monday to Thursday (Paul did not want to offend Friday showbiz columnist Baz Bamigboye by having Wicked Whispers competing with his).

Each day it included two blind items called Pssts!, which described the bad behaviour of anonymous celebrities. One particular item wondered which star, after a season in Blackpool, had impregnated one of the show girls and left her pregnant? The following day I got an email from veteran singing star Jess Conrad. 'Is it me?' he asked. It wasn't.

One of my duties was attending the daily planning meeting where department heads sat in a semicircle around Paul Dacre's antique desk struggling to come up with ideas for features.

Three months after I joined the paper (it was November), one bright spark suggested that we should highlight the disappointing sales of poppies just two weeks before Remembrance Sunday.

The editor suggested a vox pop – or, as he wittily phrased it, a vox poppy – of the assembled team. Were we wearing poppies? Most of us were in shirtsleeves with our jackets hanging on the backs of our seats at our various work stations outside Paul's office.

Pointing to sports editor Colin Gibson, Paul asked, 'Colin, are you wearing a poppy?' Colin lied: 'Yes, boss.'

Turning to me, he said, 'McWicked?' 'No, I am not, Paul,' I answered.

This triggered an eruption. 'You fucking Irish. You left the lights on in Dublin so the Germans could bomb Belfast. You refuelled the U-boats off the coast of Galway and you signed the book of condolence for Hitler at the German embassy in Dublin at the end of the war. You treacherous, treacherous Irish.'

Meekly, I explained that I hadn't even been born when Éamon de Valera stayed neutral in World War Two.

During my first summer at the *Mail*, I developed a habit of slipping away at lunchtime for a swim at the nearby Serpentine in Hyde Park. One balmy afternoon I sat in my swimsuit reading *The Guardian* when a familiar figure emerged from the water. It was fellow gossip columnist Helen Minsky. She pointed at my toes.

'Why are your toenails painted?' I looked down, baffled. I had forgotten that, weeks before, a ten-year-old had asked if she could paint my toenails different colours while I watched TV one evening. Mumbling this explanation to Minsky, I realised it sounded implausible.

Then, as September signalled the end of the Serpentine swimming season, I was sitting in the *Daily Mail* newsroom one evening with colleagues Geoffrey Levy and Richard Kay when the editor, a mug of tea in hand, came down to us for some post-first edition banter. Inevitably Ireland came up and he reprised his criticism of Irish neutrality. It was a good-natured discussion and I again stressed that I was too young to remember – not even born, in fact – de Valera pursue his misguided policy. As Paul began his journey back to his office, he turned, looked slyly at Levy and Kay to ensure their attention, and quipped, 'But who can trust an Irishman who paints his toenails?'

Then, in 2009, the recurrent nightmares of my glorious career carousel lurching to a halt became a reality.

The *Daily Mail* embarked on a draconian cost-cutting exercise. I was summoned to the office of managing editor Charles Garside to be told my sandwiches had been wrapped in a road map. He didn't quite put it like that. He told me that I was being made redundant. I was fifty-seven. I can't deny that it was a blow. For as long as I could remember I had been a well-paid, expenses-pampered hack, mostly on diaries, but I once had been a real journalist. I knew I never would be again.

The blow from the *Mail* was swiftly followed by another from Linda O'Reilly, editor of *The Anglo-Celt*, the weekly provincial in Cavan where I had started my journalistic journey in 1970. Ever since my grandfather Andrew McEntee had been indentured as an apprentice printer at the *Celt* in 1886, there had been a family connection with the paper.

My uncle had been a printer there. My father was deputy editor. My brothers Aindreas and Myles started there as trainee reporters. It tickled me to think that I, as a weekly columnist for the paper in London, was maintaining the historic family link. Not any more.

Then Sky News abruptly dropped me as their weekend newspaper reviewer. I had been doing the job for more than fifteen years and was not aware of any negative reaction. A sheepish producer muttered something about trying out more women.

I hope it was only a coincidence that my departure from Sky coincided with the arrival as breakfast anchorman of fellow Irishman Eamonn Holmes. Well-nourished Eamonn had been stung by my many references to him in print as Eamonn 'who ate all the pies' Holmes, but I had nothing to do with Eamonn's complaint to the BBC after impressionist Jon Culshaw, wearing a body suit, mimicked Eamonn on the breakfast sofa eating the furniture. The last straw for the rotund Eamonn was when Culshaw depicted him devouring diminutive jockey Frankie Dettori, saying, 'I thought it was a wee snack, I did.'

He had sued me over an inaccurate paragraph about him in Wicked Whispers. An apology to Eamonn appeared in the final column before it was axed. It coincided with Eamonn's departure from GMTV for Sky News and he rejoiced at my demise.

PART 1

BOARDING THE CAROUSEL

R eviewing my life, I sadly concede that my Irish mother would not be entirely happy with the antics and behaviour of her eldest son. I know she was unjustifiably proud of me and I just thank God she succumbed to Alzheimer's around about the time I lost the run of myself.

She died in the summer of 2015. She was ninety but had really checked out nearly a decade before when the creeping fog of Alzheimer's disease began smothering her mind. She spent the last six years of her life in Esker Lodge, a specialist home on Cavan's Cathedral Road, sitting vacant-eyed, contented, reliving her childhood on the family farm in Lavey eight miles away.

Her dreams were of a cow-dung-scented milking parlour. On a three-legged stool her robust mother sturdily extracted milk from teats into a bucket between her legs. She remembered her mother's staunch refusal to attend her wedding breakfast in Virginia in 1951. Well, she had insisted on marrying a man from the town, thwarting her mother's plan to give her decent dowry to the neighbour's child, Tommy Tierney, with his big nose, baldness and rolling acres.

Her father would object and stand up for her. But he is dead and she is in the fug of dementia. To her, Mammy and Daddy are alive forty and fifty years after they've gone. More alive than her own children.

She talked of cycling home the six miles from Jackson's Garage in Cavan, where she did the accounts. In her head she is preparing the tea in the low-ceilinged kitchen with its dry battery-powered radio, open fire and butter kept in the freezing and unused hall behind.

She couldn't remember the names of her grandchildren but she talked with great lucidity of dead brothers Mickey, Packy and Gene and sister Meg. She too is long gone.

For me, my mother died six years before we called McMahon, the undertaker. Her life force and her soul had gone from her. Just turned eighty-four, a lady who walked and talked and looked like my mother wandered the bright and warm and soothing corridors of Esker Lodge.

She was an impostor. She was not my mother.

My mother, like Elvis, had left the auditorium. She had gone elsewhere. Not suddenly or dramatically. Her death notice had not appeared in the newspapers, had not been macabrely enunciated on the local radio station, which broadcast the local death notices she so enjoyed listening to before her illness.

'Guess who's dead?' she'd ask when I called from London. She'd have gleaned all the most recent departures from Northern Sound or during her frequent trips to Dunnes Stores up the street. And if I had made the mistake of calling during the televised golf at home or abroad she would make it palpably clear that it was not a good time.

Young McIlroy's US Open triumph would have been a prime example. Now it doesn't matter. Her golf clubs are mothballed, the winning Waterford Crystal four ball prizes are no longer dusted.

I miss her wit and her sense of fun and her total engagement with the life of a small town. When the euro replaced the Irish pound in 2000, she declared, 'Now why couldn't they have waited until all the old people were dead first?'

It sneaked up on her and us. Our father died aged eighty-six in 1997. Younger by more than twenty years, she was devoted to him. My sister recalls her in old age ironing his shorts and vests and kissing each one. But there was a sense of relief that his final illness and departure happened just in time for her to assume the captaincy of the local golf club.

And when I read my father's last pocket diary, there was one dramatic entry after four months of silence: STROKE! It was in my mother's handwriting.

She had always been eccentric. But perhaps because she was good-looking and charming her curious manner with people was always excused. 'This is my son John, of whom I am extremely proud,' she would declare in bars and restaurants from Cavan to Dublin to London. I once in print eulogised late-night hot ham sandwiches from Monaghan's pub in Kells restoring famished McEntees en route from the airport to Cavan for the wedding of my brother Desmond.

On my next trip home, she somehow engineered a visit to Monaghan's at the top of the hill in Kells. 'Is Mrs Monaghan about?' she asked politely but insistently. When she appeared, my mother immediately launched upon her excruciatingly embarrassing mantra. Pointing at me, she declared, 'This is my son John, who wrote about your sandwiches.' I instantly bolted for the door like one of Aidan O'Brien's thoroughbreds and joined my father, who had seen it coming, on the doorstep outside.

My mother, Judy, was beautiful and daft. Not daft in the sense of mentally unstable. Eccentric more like. Brought up on a farm by a patrician widowed mother, she simply thought and acted differently. Take her performance when my father Andy died.

I had returned from London – my home since 1975 – for his funeral. He had been waked and buried and I, the eldest son, opened the front door of our terraced home in Cavan to a local priest, Fr Abie McGrath. He had come to sympathise. I continued my journey to the hired car parked at the footpath. I drove to Dublin airport eighty miles away to catch my flight to London.

Before boarding, I telephoned home to bid a farewell to my mother. My younger brother Dessie answered the telephone. 'You won't believe what happened after you left, John. McGrath sat down and drank most of a bottle of brandy and talked and talked.'

When he finally raised himself on his hind legs to leave, my mother gave him a £20 note to say a Mass for the repose of my father's soul. She led him to the door. He dropped dead on the street.

'Judy ran after him and got down beside him on the

street,' explained Dessie. 'Mrs Gaffey came out of her house next door. "I'm a nurse," she said. A fecking nurse! She must be eighty. Anyway, she felt for McGrath's pulse and pronounced him dead. Now she's going around telling everyone how Judy McEntee tried to resuscitate McGrath. Resuscitate him! She was feckin' looking for the twenty pounds. She never found it. God, she's annoyed.'

Her admirable religious belief manifested itself after she appeared for the second time on RTÉ's National Lottery show *Wheel of Fortune*. She won €80,000. Afterwards, my brother Myles telephoned me in London. 'Have you heard from the mother?' he asked. 'No,' I replied. 'I won't spoil the surprise,' he said, enigmatically.

Some days later, a letter arrived at my London home, the name and address written in Judy's unmistakable copperplate.

I opened the envelope to find a religious card bearing a colour illustration of the exposed, beating heart of Jesus. On the other side was a smudged printed stamp and signature that looked as if it was a visa to somewhere like Belarus. It was signed by a priest.

The accompanying letter from Judy explained that the enclosed gift was £1,000 worth of Masses, which she had paid for and were currently being celebrated by a nominated (and well-rewarded) cleric for the salvation of my soul. I was dumbstruck. There were seven of us in the family.

Judy had handed over €7,000 of her lottery winnings to a priest – or gang of priests – who probably thought all their Christmases had come at once. I had visions of Masses being said under floodlights around the clock, the sacred Host going up and down like a fiddler's elbow.

I telephoned her: 'Did you get my letter?' she asked expectantly. I told her I had and was absolutely delighted with her incredible gift. Heaven beckoned. No lingering in the holding oven of Purgatory for me.

It was well meant and sincere. And, for a woman who was careful with money – she never had much – extraordinarily generous. The profusion of Masses, however, did not trigger an outbreak of happiness or good fortune among myself, my three brothers and three sisters.

My younger brother Aindreas has since died of a brain tumour, my lovely youngest sister Joan, a gifted lawyer, lies crippled in a hospice, the advanced grip of multiple sclerosis creeping through her limbs. Three of our marriages, including mine, have ended and my middle sister Grainne has become mesmerised working for a fraudulent healer in Brazil.

And, shortly after her windfall, my brilliant, vivacious mother left the terrestrial plane for Planet Dementia.

Innocently racist – she had never met a 'coloured' person – she recoiled in horror when, bringing breakfast on a tray to my ten-year-old son Paul and his cousin Rory, she found them watching Michael Jackson cavorting on MTV.

'It's a black fella!' she declared in horror, suddenly lifting the empty tray to shield the boys' gaze from the TV screen. And when Michael was joined by his brothers dancing and singing on the TV, she exclaimed, 'Jesus, there's more of them!'

Even in my early childhood, her eccentricity was manifest. On the eve of my ninth Christmas, my father bought her a new electric cooker. It was fitted with a timer and he explained that she could put the family turkey in the oven before retiring to bed on Christmas Eve, setting the timer to start cooking at 8 a.m. on Christmas morning.

Us children had already been up for hours after tearing open the wrappings on Santa's offerings when my mother appeared in her dressing gown at 7.55 a.m.

Silently she pulled up a chair and sat by the cooker. On the dot of eight the timer went ping, the oven light came on and the turkey started roasting. She carefully replaced the chair at the kitchen table and returned to bed satisfied.

And, more than five years after her mother, my granny,

had died in 1967, I discovered, in a drawer in the dining-room sideboard, a cluster of half a dozen tiny white quail-like eggs. They were carefully wrapped in linen. I brought them out to the kitchen and asked my mother, 'What are these?' She jumped up and quickly snatched the eggs.

She was angry. Replacing them lovingly in their hiding place, she explained that each weekend when we visited Granny, she always returned to the town with half a dozen fresh eggs given to her by her mother from her productive hens. These shrunken eggs were the last offering from her mother before Granny succumbed to a stroke and died.

After my father's death in 1997, she became even more eccentric. Reasonably well provided for, she still accepted an offer of free coal from the local charity, the St Vincent de Paul Society. When I gently suggested that the coal might better be allocated to poorer residents of Cavan, she insisted, 'I'm entitled to it.'

And even after she abandoned the open-coal fire in the sitting room for a gas appliance with make-believe flames, she continued to allow the charity coal to stockpile in the shed at the back of the house. At the time of her death, she had acquired enough coal to survive an Arthur Scargill-inspired miners' strike.

And somehow she had wangled a pension from my father's membership of the National Union of Journalists (NUJ). Again, this regular injection of funds should have been earmarked for the needy dependents of deceased NUJ members. Initially it was paid in sterling. After two years it reverted to the less valuable euro. Judy called me: 'John, can you get on to the NUJ and tell them to pay the pension in sterling. Tell them I can't afford to run a big house and a car and pay for golf on the euros they're sending me.'

There was no point in trying to explain that the NUJ would not take too kindly to discovering that Mrs McEntee had a mortgage-free home, could afford a motor car and was a former president of the golf club where she played regularly.

In 2007, a small house fire was turned into an inferno when Judy poured water over the TV after it started emitting smoke. She was rescued but was more annoyed about the destruction of an ancient and ugly rubber mat in the hall that my late father had acquired with coupons from the John Player fags he smoked in the '50s.

During renovations, we moved her temporarily into a nearby nursing home, Esker Lodge. Little did we know she was soon to spend her last befuddled years there.

I came home from London to see her. She seemed the

same bright, vivacious, people-loving mater of old. I'd booked a table for supper at Seán Quinn's Slieve Russell Hotel twelve miles away. We were running late.

She'd forgotten her cardigan, then she had to help a fellow inmate who'd fallen out of his wheelchair. Finally she emerged. In the car park was a lone, tall woman standing, de Valera-like, obviously waiting to be collected.

As I held the car door open for my eternally affable mother, she walked away from the car and addressed the stranger. 'Did you hear about the fire?' She then regaled this total stranger with a twenty-minute account of the drama. Eventually I got her into the car. Her response? 'I wish people wouldn't ask me about the fire.'

And so she returned home. But, unbeknownst to us, she was becoming acutely forgetful, turning up twelve hours late for morning Mass at the local cathedral. She was also wandering about the town asking strangers who she was. My sister Ann came home from Boston. On the morning of her return, Judy fell in the kitchen and broke her arm. She was distressed and confused. It wasn't just the arm. She was diagnosed with Alzheimer's.

And then, over the most heart-breaking eighteen months, she was confined to a home she did all she could to escape from. Twice she broke through the emergency exit and was caught in the fields heading homewards. My sainted brother Dessie had to deny her time after time the key to the front door of her own home. In the meantime, her clothes were stolen frequently, a common practice among those *sans* reason.

She was still mostly compos mentis and this was awful for a dignified lady to bear. 'Why am I here?' she plaintively asked.

Her dignity and high self-esteem were gradually eroded. I came home in the bleak winter of 2009 and took her out. Driving back to the home, she asked me politely for the key of the front door. I declined. In the hallway of the home, as I removed her suede coat, hat and scarf for safekeeping, she pointed to a notice on the closed door. 'What does that say, John?' she asked innocently. I opened the door and walked out to read it. She was instantly at my elbow. 'John, take me home, please, take me home.' Tears welled up in my eyes as I gently led her back into the hypnotic warmth of the home. I left her there.

Shortly after that, there were no more pleas for her door key. No tricks to escape, no plan to get away. She simply didn't want to leave. It is the way of the world: drugs and dementia. The gentle chemical tip-tap had taken over. Not quite *One Flew Over the Cuckoo's Nest*, but close. No cruel nurses or rebellious Jack Nicholson, but she had been subdued and tamed nonetheless. Bed by eight. Some bingo and Ludo and painting. Lots of tea and biscuits and cake. Soothing. And then there is the meal she must prepare for her long-dead father and mother. 'Can't speak. Who are you? Must get home to Mammy and Daddy. They are waiting.'

By her ninetieth birthday in April 2015, the light had dimmed to a speck. We gathered from London, Boston, Brazil, Dublin. We celebrated with a Mass and cake. Her nephew, Fr Johnny Cusack, went through the holy ritual with my mother barking, 'Who are you? I shouldn't be here!' until, as he proffered the sacred Host to her lips, she smiled and said, 'Hello, God.'

At the funeral in June 2015 in Killygarry graveyard in Cavan, my cousin John observed that while the Irish were generally useless at managing, they were brilliant at funerals.

John's astute assessment was right. It wasn't grieving so much as a celebration. My prediction of a poor turn-out was, like my racing tips, widely off the mark.

In London, you die. No one, including family, is keen to see the remains. Ten days later, the funeral cortège snakes anonymously through busy streets to a crematorium. In Ireland, it is different. People want to see the body. They want to talk about the person who has died. They offer condolences simply and sincerely.

The honour and respect accorded my mother astonished her English-born grandchildren and others unfamiliar with the Irish way of death. With the majority of her contemporaries and friends dead, as I say, I had expected a small turnout.

I knew she was a splendid woman, but had no idea how many other people shared that view. At McMahon's funeral home, where she reposed in a top-of-the-range oak coffin, insisted upon by my grief-stricken brother Dessie, prayers were organised the day after her death on Wednesday.

They were hugely oversubscribed. Dessie suggested that the huge turnout was, perhaps, down to the presence of her brother Johnny Cusack, the great Cavan footballer and one of the tiny band of Breifne men in possession of an All-Ireland winner's medal. That was part of it.

But the following evening, at the removal of her remains to the local cathedral, there was an even larger throng. So much so that the undertaker John McMahon intervened to urge a speeding up of sympathising. The queue of mourners snaked out the door and back to the old Cavan Railway Station, now the offices of the local newspaper *The Anglo-Celt*.

At Cavan Cathedral we carried her in. The length of time praying was dwarfed by the two hours of hand-shaking as even more people uttered the mantra 'Very sorry for your troubles'.

On Friday, it was *Groundhog Day* at the actual funeral. At the end of a glorious funeral Mass conducted by Fr Johnny Cusack, Dessie asked me to thank our mother's carers at Esker Lodge. I recalled that she was blissfully unaware of her own worth.

One of her weekly treats was a night at the bingo in the Town Hall, followed by a gin and tonic in the Farnham Hotel with her sisters-in-law, Anna Conlan and Josephine McEntee, and a golfing pal, Margaret English.

On this particular night, it was raining cats and dogs and a particular dog, a cocker spaniel called Mixer, owned by surgeon Maloney, waddled into the Farnham Bar and made straight for Judy.

This was understandable, as the dog spent all his time in Judy's kitchen being fed and looked after. He promptly shook himself dry, drenching Mrs English. A bit of a battleaxe, she ordered Judy to take the dog home. Judy protested that the owner of the dog, surgeon Maloney, was standing at the bar. She waved hopefully in his direction and mouthed hello. He studiously ignored her. Judy was obliged to leave her drink and, in pouring rain, walk Mixer past the old surgical hospital to Maloney's house (now the site of Dunnes Stores). She closed the gate, leaving Mixer in the shelter of the garage, and quickly returned to the Farnham. No sooner had she sat down than Mixer waddled in and repeated his exercise, drenching Mrs English yet again. This time Judy got up, walked Mixer back and went home defeated.

And still the sympathisers surged forward. After the funeral Mass, a further two hours of handshaking and good wishes ensued. So much so that when eventually it came to an end, the undertaker required two more tall McEntees to help carry Judy from the cathedral. I couldn't find my two 6 ft-plus sons Jack and Paul. They had slipped away with their cousin Rory to do shots at Donohoe's bar.

The Garda closed Church Street to allow the family to walk behind the hearse in sunshine to Judy's house. As we stood in silence outside the family home she had occupied for more than fifty years, my sisters Ann and Grainne vanished in the front door. I assumed it was a comfort stop. 'No,' Ann explained at the cemetery, 'We had a large gin and tonic each.'

One hundred people surrounded the grave as Judy's nephew uttered the final prayers of farewell. In sunshine we stood for an hour afterwards remembering her. As

Dessie said, 'God, our mammy loved funerals. She'd have loved this one. Say not in grief that Judy is no more / But live in Thankfulness that she was.'

She also loved her children and, too late, I thank her for an idyllic childhood. I was born in 1952, the eldest of four boys and three girls, and it was my mother who dominated our childhood. My father, already into his forties when I appeared, was a shadowy figure. His life revolved around a quartet of work at *The Anglo-Celt*, where he was deputy editor, frequent golf and fly-fishing and the pub.

We spent much of our early summers with Granny Cusack, Judy's mother. In my mind Judy's home farm located eight miles from our house in the town remains a magical place. Her mother may have been stern, but to me and my brothers – the girls hadn't appeared yet – she was adorable. Dressed in a stained woollen jumper, black skirt and wellingtons, with giant breasts sagging to her waist, she presided over a two-storey farmhouse devoid of plumbing or running water.

'When I grow up,' I boasted to Granny Cusack, 'I am going to be a plumber and I'll put in taps and a sink and a bath and toilet.'

She ruffled my hair and chuckled. Water came in buckets drawn from a spring well half a mile from the house.

What Granny and her bachelor sons Johnny and Gene did for bodily functions was left to the imagination.

As an eight-year-old I remember sharing a large bed in the bedroom over the kitchen with my younger brothers Aindreas, Myles and toddler Dessie. The window over-looked what was called the front street, a concreted patio outside the never-used front door. All traffic came through the back street and into the kitchen.

During the night, all of us had calls of nature. We discovered a Victorian wooden chair that had a hidden toilet bowl under the wooden, hinged seat. It was a commode.

All four us, in turn, eagerly clambered onto the primitive toilet and made deposits in the commode. Afterwards, as the oldest, I lay awake wondering how to dispose of the human waste. It was unthinkable to mention the matter to my granny or uncles. Toilet, willies and all references to bodily functions were not matters up for discussion with Granny.

I rose at dawn and removed the laden bowl from the chair and tossed the contents out the window onto the concrete front patio, leaving daubs of excrement on the outside wall and kitchen window.

I was blissfully unaware that Uncle Johnny was an even earlier riser. He was chomping through his breakfast soda bread and tea at the table beside the kitchen window below. He gaped at the sudden descent from heaven of ripe turds from four nephewly bottoms. He wasn't pleased.

Bolting the wooden stairs, he burst into the room to peer at four supposedly sleeping figures in the giant bed. 'Who threw the shite out the window?' he roared. Silence. My eyelids fluttered as he roared the question a second time, followed by, 'Right, yez bucks.'

In my mind, in slow motion, I can still see his approaching boot as it landed under the bed and sent the mattress heavenwards. Dessie began to cry as Johnny pulled me by my right ear from the bed. 'Get out there and scrape all that shite up, you little bollocks.'

I duly did. A week later, hair oiled and angelic, we were paraded in Granny's parlour for what was called a spree to celebrate the ordination of our cousin Fr Johnny Cusack. Yanked again by the ear, Uncle Johnny introduced me to the new priest. 'This is the buck who threw the shit out of the window.' This was followed by a tractor engine ignition noise that passed for Johnny's laughter. I was mortified.

Johnny was kind to us and his fury over my waste disposal arrangement was justified and understandable. Thankfully, I escaped his wrath for another toilet prank.

I persuaded baby Dessie, new to the art of toilet training, that a knot hole in the wooden floor of Gene's bedroom above the parlour was the lavatory, or, as I explained it, 'the wee wee hole'.

Painstakingly, assisted by brother Aindreas, I manoeuvred Dessie's flaccid willy into the hole and allowed him to relieve himself. Over the course of one summer holiday, this became Dessie's regular port of call. In time, the plaster on the ceiling became discoloured with Dessie's urine. We couldn't blame the plumbing. There were no pipes in the house. Conveniently, the chunky ceiling plaster waited until our departure home for the new school term before it collapsed on the mahogany dining-room table below.

By the early '60s, most country homes had only just received electricity – some inhabitants naively taping over sockets to prevent the 'escape' of the current. Only a very few had bathrooms and indoor toilet facilities. Toilets were still in their infancy in rural Cavan.

As we lived in the town, we had an indoor toilet. But for two adults and seven children, this was often disastrously inadequate. My permanently middle-aged father, a man of precise habits, always rose at 9.30 a.m. and retired to the thunderbox with editions of the previous day's *Evening Press* and *Herald*. His evacuation always took more than half an hour. Often there was a queue of cross-legged daughters sometimes supplemented with an anxious wife. In desperation, the females of the family sometimes had to resort to a tin can in the back shed.

My London-based uncle Kevin – more of him soon – spent his last holidays vacationing at his sister-in-law's remote, tin-roofed farmhouse in the district of Maghera near Virginia in County Cavan. The cottage did not have a toilet. One summer morning, Kevin, a short, roly-poly figure plagued by varicose veins, chose the hay field abutting the laneway to the house for his morning clear-out. Kevin dropped his trousers anklewards and squatted. In the tall, un-mown grass, only his head was visible from the road. Unfortunately, the local postman, cycling towards the house to deliver a letter, spotted Kevin's hair-oiled comb-over and red, straining countenance. Dismounting his bike, he hailed him: 'Good morning, Kevin. Home from England?'

A startled Kevin replied from the long grass that he was. His monosyllabic answer did not have the desired effect.

Leaning on the handlebars, the postman reminisced about his brief, long-ago experience of London and, acknowledging grunts and ayes from Kevin, proceeded to bring him up to speed on all local developments, including the welfare of his family and the shambles of

Taoiseach Jack Lynch's government as well as the state of the roads.

'He must have talked for half an hour,' complained Kevin. 'I couldn't stand up or he'd have known I was having a shite. With my varicose veins it was excruciating. When he finally got back on the bike I fell over into the grass.'

I can talk. Long before, as a relatively recently toilet-trained child at infant school at the Poor Clare Convent in Cavan, I regularly suffered in silence when Mother Imelda left the class for half an hour. There was no one to see my raised hand and grant permission for a trip to the school toilet. I wasn't alone in squirming, occasionally unable to hold on and staining the wooden floor with warm wee. Once my classmate Eamon Cusack nudged me and pointed, giggling, at the floor. Like steaming chicken nuggets, a trio of rounded turds sat accusingly, cooling on the planks. Silently and shame-facedly, I retrieved the deposits and placed them back carefully in my underpants until the nun returned to release me.

What is it with the Irish and bodily functions? While London correspondent of the *Irish Press* in the late '70s, I pointed my notebook in the direction of a Brixton pub to interview writer Dermot Healy. Dermot, author of the brilliant memoir *The Bend for Home*, was well known in the alehouse. We talked and drank pints of Guinness all day. The following day, peering at my porter-stained notes, I telephoned the Brixton pub to speak to Dermot and ask him for help in deciphering what he'd actually said.

Summoned to the telephone atop the bar, he said, 'Hold on a minute.' The line went dead. I could hear the murmur of conversations, glasses clinking, darts thudding into a nearby board, the general hum of a busy pub. I waited and waited and waited. It was a full five minutes before Dermot's voice asked, 'Now, how can I help you?' I asked him where on earth he'd been. 'Having a shite,' he answered brightly. 'I thought it was grand that you were here waiting for me at the bar.'

Whirling back to the clock to my childhood days in Lavey, my adventure with the commode had become one of Uncle Johnny's favourite anecdotes. He was a fabled Gaelic footballer who had played for his county in Cavan's golden era.

In one All-Ireland final at Dublin's Croke Park, Johnny missed an open goal. Prone to depression, he suffered a nervous breakdown. Berthed briefly in an institution in Dublin, his sister Judy, my mother, brought him a bottle containing holy water from St Dymphna's Well, which was at a shrine a mile from the family farmstead. St Dymphna was the patron saint of the mentally ill.

Subsequently Johnny threw himself from the second-floor window of the asylum, breaking an arm and a leg. My mother remarked that if it wasn't for the holy water he would have died. I wondered aloud why the holy water hadn't prevented him from jumping in the first place.

Johnny's brother Gene was our favourite. We didn't know at the time, but Gene's good humour was often down to his weakness for strong drink.

Returning from Brady's bar in Stradone, he would take us to the hayshed and insist we watch him stand on his head. His real motive was to allow us to plunder the straw for all the coins that cascaded from his upside-down pockets while he performed his party trick.

Gene bestowed one magic memory on my brothers and I.

'Do you want to see my money-making machine?' he would ask. He would then lead us surreptitiously through the dark and dank interior of the old disused family watermill with its rotting wooden wheel and lingering scent of flour.

His magic ritual was to put his finger to his lips, asking for secrecy as he started an old threshing machine

with a canvas conveyor belt. As we watched the throbbing machine in wonder, he would slip three half-crowns
– then a substantial treasure – onto the belt and enjoy
our goggle-eyed delight at the appearance of the loot on
the conveyer of his 'money-making machine'.

I subsequently went back to school with a swagger,
knowing that, should financial catastrophe descend on
the McEntee family, I had the means to alleviate it. Gene
would surely produce enough half-crowns to save us
from penury.

Despite these high-spirited displays, there was an air
of melancholy about Gene, the cause of which I only
learned in adulthood. In love with a neighbour's daughter, his mother banned him from seeing her. Years before,
her parents had bid for the watermill subsequently purchased by my grandparents. They drove the price high
enough to cause the Cusacks serious financial problems.
My granny never forgave them.

When Gene walked his bicycle to the end of the
meandering lane to meet his sweetheart on the road, his
mother frequently emerged from the hedge to curse the
lovebirds and demand that Gene return home. He was
dispossessed from her will. No land beckoned for Gene.
When the love of his life got to hear that Gene was land-
less, she married someone else.

Gene then bought his own neighbouring farm, continuing to live at home as a bachelor. But on his two-mile evening trudge from the farm to home, a ritual developed with a widow who ran the local shop. Bewhiskered Mrs Kathleen Tierney invited Gene in for tea. She would wait at the door of her shop, with its tin Gaelic advertisement for Sweet Afton on the outside wall, and lure the younger farmer into her parlour. He eventually married her and ended his days a teetotal miser, the laughter and magic of the money-making machine a distant memory.

I once accompanied Uncle Johnny and a randy cow across the river to Murray's farm, where a bull awaited. As we trudged through the rush-filled field with the cow on the end of a rope held by Johnny, the roaring of the distant bull aroused Daisy. She began to canter and then run towards the noise. Johnny held on gamely to the rope uttering curses – 'Ye whore's melt. Ye feckin' bollocks' – as his bottom slid along the ground.

It was like waterskiing without the boat or the water. Uncle Johnny was almost horizontal. A trickle of coins exited his pockets as he sped along behind the cow. Finally on the river bank, he subdued her and then realised that all the money he was carrying had fallen out in the few hundred yards of flattened grass and rushes in the path forged by the rampant cow. Although it was twilight, I was dragooned into helping as he retraced his steps, painstakingly peering at the ground in search of his lost florins, half-crowns, sixpence and three-penny pieces. It took an hour and was dark when we resumed our journey, all coins accounted for.

The arrival of our baby sister Ann meant that our adventures with Granny were supplemented with a nappy-wearing baby. To help with the washing of the endless Terry nappies, my mother had her nearly new Servis top-loading washing machine dispatched to Lavey by the *Anglo-Celt* delivery van.

Granny stared at the machine in her stone-floored kitchen as if it had been the spaceship discarded by a visiting alien. Remember, this grand lady had only just come to terms with electricity. She had a Eureka moment and ordered her son Johnny to fill the washing machine with milk. She'd worked out that the cleaning process was identical to churning. She made butter. I was sworn to secrecy. But the butter had done little to improve the running of the Servis's motor. And I'm sure Granny's butter must have had nappy pins and at least a few buttons hidden in it when it was finally extracted.

The death of our granny in the mid-'60s ended the joy of our annual Lavey idyll. Johnny had married an attractive and feisty local teacher called Anna who was not as tolerant of rampaging nephews from the nearby town. On my first post-Granny visit to Lavey, I was put to work on the farm. By then I was fourteen.

One daily task was to mix the buckets of pig feed and trudge the half-mile to the old mill to feed the sow and her thirteen baby bonhams located in an outhouse adjacent to the mill race. After much rainfall, the small stream was a raging torrent heading downwards towards the rotting timber watermill.

I opened the shed door and a carpet of hungry beige baby piglets stampeded towards me. Before I could close the door behind me, four had managed to scamper between my legs and escape. They headed straight for the river. Leaving the remaining pigs and the beached mother along with the buckets, I closed the door behind me and raced across the field to retrieve the pigs. I managed to catch two and return them to their mother.

Searching further downstream beyond the mill I found the other two lying sideways floating on the water. They had drowned. Catastrophe. I lifted each baby pig and returned them to their mother. I carefully placed both deceased babies alongside their mum, their lifeless snouts nudging her teats.

I returned to the farm house that evening and did not tell either Anna or Johnny the drama of the drowning.

The following day Johnny discovered the dead bonhams. Under interrogation I feigned ignorance, suggesting helpfully that they may have suffered nocturnal heart attacks. 'Heart attacks?' roared Johnny. 'They were fucking soaking wet!'

It was my last holiday in Lavey. In subsequent years, sitting sardine-like in the back of the family Ford Anglia en route to the seaside at Bettystown, I would glance nostalgically as my father passed the side road leading to my mother's old homestead and remember happy times.

Just further along the Dublin road stood the substantial dwelling of Tommy Tierney, the farmer my mother had spurned to marry the love of her life. She would always point at the two-storey house with its pristine sheds and outhouses and declare, quite illogically, 'John, you could have had all that.'

All of my brothers and two of my sisters were born at home. The youngest, Joan, was born in Lisdarn Hospital and I, the first, emerged from the local County Home, previously Cavan workhouse. Sounds Dickensian, I know, but it was a decent hospital.

My father did not see his firstborn for over a month – he was in a Dublin hospital recovering from what we now call deep-vein thrombosis. He was charmed with his bright, attentive new son called John Andrew Francis.

This was unfortunate for his next son, Aindreas. He was born at home while my father and Dr Jack Sullivan drank whiskey in the dining room downstairs. When midwife Mrs Dale Jenkins trudged down the stairs to tell him Judy had been safely delivered of a boy, he dashed to the bedside. He was appalled at the still-damp miniature Winston Churchill presented by Judy.

Aindreas's arrival was to have depressing repercussions in my early teens, when all the resentment of being displaced as the only child manifested itself in bullying, ostracisation and cruelty. There were five more children: Myles, Desmond, Ann, Grainne and Joan.

Both Ann and Grainne were born at home over Christmas holidays in 1962 and 1963. As the day of Ann's arrival loomed, Aindreas and I were dispatched to Auntie Maud, my mother's older sister in Dublin, seventy miles away.

While we grew fond of Maud and her husband Peter, we were not keen to repeat the experience. She had married late and their small terraced house in Drumcondra was a work in progress, as was their roly-poly new baby Patrick. New father Pete, a bald-headed carpenter, was yet to understand the sensitivities of little boys.

I was barely ten and Aindreas eight when, on our first evening in Drumcondra, Peter invited us into the freezing back garden (it was the coldest winter in twenty years) to explain our sleeping arrangements.

Pointing his torch towards a snow-covered shed with a lopsided door precariously clinging to one hinge, he said, 'You'll be in here, boys.' With mounting horror we peered into the bleak interior with its broken furniture, heap of coal and rotting newspapers.

Back in the warm kitchen, he continued the torture: 'I think I've got rid of all the rats in the shed.' We gulped like cartoon characters in our favourite comic, *The Beano*.

Then, pointing at a crest-shaped scar on his right cheek, Pete explained gravely, 'I got that from one of the rats in the shed. I cornered him and the bollocks leaped at me and bit my face. He got lockjaw and I couldn't pull him off.' Warming to his theme, he added, 'I had to catch the bus to the Mater (Hospital) holding the rat. They managed to prise him off and kill him.'

Andy and I were now literally retching in terror. 'Mammy, come and rescue us!' I screamed inside.

Then Maud, a large-boned, jolly-faced figure in floral apron (who until then had been enjoying her husband's frightful fantasy), snapped, 'Peter, stop frightening the boys!'

She beckoned us towards the downstairs front room. Inside was an unfolded sofa bed decked out neatly with sheets, blankets, two pillows and an eiderdown.

'You'll be sleeping in here,' she soothed.

Almost tearful with gratitude, we hugged Maud's middle and then ran back into the kitchen, spontaneously performing a jig of joy around the seated Pete. Both of us then drummed his bald head with our hands in thanks and delight.

Pete's smile faded. 'I wouldn't do that if I were you.' We stopped, anxiety suddenly resurfacing. 'Why not, Uncle Peter?' Gravely he explained, 'My father was bald too. I did that one night before going to bed. I woke up in the morning and all my hair was lying on the sheet. I was completely bald. I was about the same age as you,' pointing at his open-mouthed nephews.

The evening was destroyed. We retired to bed, the room dimly lit from a street light outside. Sleep was fitful. Both of us awoke frequently throughout the night to check the state of our hair. Was it still in place? Were we now bald?

And Pete had added a detail to further distress us. 'Everyone at school laughed at me for being bald. My father got me a wig. But one day the other boys snatched it and threw it on a bonfire.'

Our young lives were in ruins. Bald at ten! What would Mammy say?

In the morning we awoke to find no discarded hair

on the pillow. Fifty years later I still have my hair and, to his dying day in 2005, so had my dear brother Andy.

Until my mid-teens, August was spent amid the sand dunes of Bettystown about sixty miles from the inland town of Cavan. In the months before our vacation, my father would abstain from his usual evening visits to Eddie Gorman's bar to help pay for the rent of a galvanised roofed house near the beach.

After driving us to Bettystown in a car borrowed from Miss Joan O'Hanlon, a director of the weekly newspaper where he toiled, Andy would spend the weekend with us by the seaside. Then he would return to work, visiting us on subsequent weekends.

Though married with a large family, he still lived the idyllic life of a bachelor. Work was not sufficiently burdensome to prohibit afternoons at the local golf links. Evenings were spent over bottles of Guinness and half-bottles of Robin Redbreast whiskey in Gorman's.

And between May and September he was not to be seen as he chased trout with the mayfly and cast his flies over all the rivers and lakes in a county boasting more water than anywhere else in Ireland.

I was put off fly fishing for life by the age of ten because of a ritual encouraged by my mother and enthusiastically embraced by my father. Andy's angling club had boats on Annagh Lake, located six miles from our home, from which he nightly fished for rainbow trout.

I was appointed oarsman and on the drive to Annagh he would stop the Ford Anglia in the village of Butlersbridge to collect the boat keys from Mrs Barclays in the village sweet shop. As I sat in the car, he would purchase an indeterminate number of long, thin, blue-wrapped Cadbury's Dairy Milk chocolate bars and hide them in the various pockets of his fishing jacket.

Over the next three hours, as I rowed the wooden boat in descending darkness in pursuit of the gulping sounds and disturbed water of a rising trout, he would casually throw a bar of chocolate towards me onto the floor of the boat. There was very little conversation. My mind was preoccupied, wondering how many bars Andy had left.

Whether he had caught his quota of three fish or not, our homeward journey was always the same. He would park the Ford Anglia outside Con Smyth's bar in Butlersbridge, tell me he wouldn't be long, walk the short distance down the street to Mrs Barclays' shop and drop the boat keys through the letterbox. Then he would walk back up past the car and disappear into the smoky, dim-lit interior of Smyth's front bar.

After forty minutes sitting in the worn brown leather of the front seat, my imagination would have conjured up a violent attack on my father. An angry farmer or irate fellow angler annoyed at his boasting of captured fish had punched him to the ground. Now he was being kicked about the floor, drunken strangers laughing at him.

I sounded the horn on the steering wheel. Beep. Beep. Beep.

My father would emerge from Smyth's front door, often carrying a packet of Tayto crisps. 'What's wrong? Are you all right?' his Smithwick ale-scented voice would ask. Then he would throw the crisps through the open driver's door, saying, 'Here, have these. I'll only be a couple of minutes.'

He was always more cheerful on the last leg of the journey to Church Street, where we lived. It was usually near midnight when my mother would ruffle my hair in the hall and ask brightly, 'Did you have a good time with your daddy?'

He meant well and was frequently cajoled into making the three-hour journey by road for a day trip to Bundoran on the rugged Atlantic coast of County Donegal. Invariably we would sit squashed in the back of the rain-drenched Ford Anglia staring out at the Atlantic breakers.

One of these visits was just after we had acquired our first television set, a nineteen-inch black-and-white Bush.

Andy and I became immediate telly addicts, enjoying *The Lone Ranger* and *I Love Lucy*. RTÉ hadn't started broadcasting and the spare channel carried a test card picture of a Connemara cottage. We stared for hours at the monochrome cottage, convinced we could see activity through the tiny windows. A farmer, his wife, children, even a donkey.

One grim day after my dad parked beside Bundoran's windswept and sodden Esplanade, having driven across Glen Gap with the mandatory stops to vomit on the roadside, Andy and I rebelled. 'We want to go home and watch telly,' we wailed. I could see my father's neck turning crimson in rage. He started the car. 'Right, right, we're going home.' And we did.

After his death, I leafed through the bundle of pocket diaries he'd kept. There was little about the birth, upbringing and achievements of his children. Regular cryptic entries over more than four decades were: 'nine holes, two trout, diahrrea two tabs [medicine], nj [no jar].'

Back home after holidays, school resumed with the curate's egg of teachers from the order of De La Salle brothers. I say curate's egg because some of the brothers were good but at least one of them was very, very bad – as in, malevolent.

Like most mothers, mine had a soft spot for the

handsome Brother Francis, similar in looks to the yet-to-be-born George Clooney. I was one of his favourites and, through his patronage, I had obtained a place on the football team and membership to the school flageolet band.

It was his replacement, Brother Timothy, who first noticed the oddness. He had taken over stewardship of the band after the sudden and mysterious departure of Francis.

Putting the existing band members through their paces, he was astonished to discover I couldn't actually play. Brother Francis hadn't felt it necessary for his gangly ten-year-old protégé to learn the flute to be in the band. And I didn't need football skills to be on the class team.

Brother Francis would now be called a paedophile, a term not in use in Cavan in the late '50s. My inclusion in the band and the football team were rewards for allowing Francis to interfere with me.

The only criterion for selection seems to have been looks. If you were plug ugly or, as some of the poorer boys were, filthy, you were in no danger of the discreet summons to Francis's knee during class.

Francis taught us arithmetic, English, Irish, geography, history and religious instruction. Aged eight, it was considered quite a privilege to be selected for Francis's sexual attention. I, like my friends, knew it was wrong, but we were not then sexually awake. What he did, and we allowed him to do, was simply naughty – like wetting your trousers.

His technique never varied. A maths test or essay would be signalled on the blackboard and it was heads down as we scribbled feverishly. 'John,' he would say, beckoning with his finger as he sat behind his desk at the top of the classroom, 'can you come up here for a word?'

It didn't seem odd being asked to sit on his soutane-shrouded lap. 'Your mother', he would begin, 'is very keen for you to join the band. Would you like that?'

'Yes, Brother,' I would answer as his right hand wandered up my exposed knee towards the hem of my short trousers. 'Well, I can arrange that,' Francis would whisper as his hand reached my thigh and disappeared under the trews. Reaching my dormant penis, he would stroke and twiddle, all the time droning on about my progress in the class. I was too pre-pubescent to be aroused, but recall the acute sense of danger and illicitness. I can't remember if Francis was aroused beneath the folds of his black soutane, but I wouldn't have recognised an erection if it had slapped me in the face.

The 'chat' might last fifteen minutes before I was told to return to my seat.

My friends Barry and Brendan, among others, had similar experiences. After class we would congregate in the cloakroom to discuss and giggle about what had happened.

There was an unspoken rule that we didn't tell our parents. I, like the other chosen recipients of Francis's favours, did extremely well academically. But my lack of skill on the football field was there for all to see. My mother considered Francis almost a saint for his efforts to turn me into a footballer. When she saw the band perform she had no idea her son was merely twiddling his fingers over a silent flageolet.

The boys who were not sexually fiddled with were subject to regular beatings. One, I recall, was ordered to drop his trousers in front of the entire class while Brother Francis whacked him on the bottom with a thin cane. Throughout his ordeal the victim's stricken, weeping face stared at us. We stared mutely back, watching the brutality in a manner reminiscent of William Golding's feral schoolboys in *Lord of the Flies*.

With half of Ireland since discovering they had been abused by priests or brothers, I risk opprobrium by declaring (as I did to *The Spectator*):

> It did me no harm. No damage. No trauma. No nightmares. And unless the De La Salle order is poised

with a massive cheque to compensate me for my trauma I am willing to confess that myself and my similarly singled out classmates have grown up normally and got on with our lives. We don't yearn for an earnest documentary about our plight.

Much as I would love to be interviewed with my face pixellated blathering about the abuse so long ago, I am resigned to the reality. It didn't matter. And he was an excellent teacher to boot.

His sadistic colleague Brother Cyril inflicted more real destruction on young lives with his brutal batterings and terrifying tantrums than a millennium of penis-pulling by his pervy fellow brother.

Older pupils along the corridor received even more harsh physical punishment from Brother Cyril. Long after Brother Francis's abrupt departure, we were to learn Irish the hard way under the brutality of Brother Cyril.

Beatings were thorough and regular. A demented Gaelic nationalist, his technique was to stand before a terrified twelve-year-old, demand his answer in Irish and when the petrified and stuttering youngster faltered in his delivery, Cyril would unleash a staccato barrage of open-handed slaps on both ears. He was known to punch and to draw blood with his cane.

In my final year, Cyril taught me Irish through ritual thumpings. During one winter class he failed to notice the edge of his tatty soutane catching on the wire surround of the glowing, portable oil heater in front of the class. We watched in fascination as the cloth began to smoulder and earnestly wished for Cyril's total immolation. But then one apple-polisher raised his hand and declared in pidgin Gaelic, 'Briar, briar, ta do soutane ag tine' (Brother, brother, your soutane is on fire). Needless to say, we tortured Cyril's rescuer in the playground afterwards.

But back to Brother Francis. Eventually I confided his regular fumblings to my mother. She simply didn't believe me. She thought it was a foul slur on an excellent teacher and devout brother. But the game was up for Francis. Other mothers were being alerted by my chums and one in particular took her little darling's claims seriously enough to complain to the head brother.

Something obviously happened in the Easter holidays. We returned to discover that we were now in Brother Timothy's class. Where was our beloved Brother Francis? We were genuinely upset at his departure. We learned that he had been transferred abruptly to the De La Salle operation in South Africa.

Sex education was non-existent. I recall the assistant sacristan at the local cathedral telling dirty jokes that were completely above my head. One involved a young boy seeing his mother naked in the bathroom and asking about her pubic hair. 'What's that, Mammy?' he asked. 'That's my brush, son,' replied the mother. The child protested that it didn't have a handle. 'It will when your father gets home,' the mother responded. It was all above my head – or below my belt, even.

A magazine called *Spotlight*, which featured show bands fronted by the likes of Brendan Bowyer and Dickie Rock, regularly carried advertisements for Tampax tampons. I was completely baffled by these female contraptions that contributed to 'female hygiene'. Finally I worked it out. It dawned on me that I had never heard my mother or any other woman pass wind. These cotton-wool cylinders were sophisticated silencers, therefore, which snuffled out the sound of ladies' farts. It would be funny if it wasn't so tragic.

I found farting a source of bawdy humour and was jealous of peers who could produce more frequent or nosier explosions. But girls and women never passed wind within earshot. To her dying day, I'd never heard my mother fart.

After I left the De La Salle brothers, I managed to squeeze into St Patrick's College, a secondary school run by priests about a mile from the town of Cavan.

St Patrick's was one of the worst schools in the new Ireland. I didn't know at the time, but now, with the hindsight of age, I lament its abysmal failure towards me and legions of others. The teachers were virtually all priests, supplemented by a gaggle of civilians *sans* ambition, imagination or much ability.

Poor Father Mallon, a classical scholar with a giant stomach that prohibited sight of his feet, had the misfortune of teaching us Christian doctrine. This included a lecture on procreation very much in the birds and bees category. When Father Mallon moved on from cross-pollination to the method of delivery of human sperm, we demanded, 'Draw it on the board, Father.' I can still conjure up the image of his shaking, chalk-clutching hand trying to replicate the female vagina on the blackboard in Class Ten.

Father Mallon's failure to explain the facts of life was sufficient to allow my father to capitulate on his duty to explain precisely where his eldest son was before his birth in the local County Home before breakfast on 10 August 1952.

Pushed reluctantly into the sitting room by my mother, he coughed a few times and asked, 'Do you know anything about the facts of life?' I replied, 'Oh, yes, Father Mallon told us all about that.'

Andy was out of the door and heading for Eddie Gorman's attitude adjustment centre faster than Linford Christie. It meant that even into early adulthood I had no real understanding of the female sexual and procreation machinery.

My parents would have been better served financially sending me to learn a trade at the local technical school than opting for St Pat's. In fact, so desperate were he and my mother to extract academic achievement from their errant elder son, I was obliged to become a boarder for the last year of my sentence.

On one weekend trip home I polished off half a dozen bottles of Guinness I'd discovered under the kitchen sink. This was normally the place my father deposited Guinness when it went, as he described it, 'sour'. Basically, it was past its sell-by date.

My mother normally gave the old stout to Johnny McDonagh, an ex-British Army tramp who begged door to door. As I glugged down the Guinness, I congratulated myself on my plan. I would explain the absence of the Guinness on a sudden call to the then empty house by dear old Johnny, who was delighted to accept the half-dozen bottles of porter.

On my next trip home, I was sitting at the kitchen table when my father asked about the missing Guinness.

'Oh, I gave the bottles to Johnny McDonagh,' I replied brightly. My father said nothing. After finishing his lunch, he left the table in silence and returned to work.

My mother said, 'You fool. Johnny McDonagh died three weeks ago.'

My recollections of St Pat's are blighted by the experience of a classmate, J. P. Breen, from Kinawley in County Fermanagh. He was only twelve and still in short trousers when his parents crossed the border and deposited him as a first-year boarder in St Pat's.

As a product of the Northern Ireland educational system, his primary school had not taught him a word of Irish, a subject necessary to pass any state exam in the glorious republic.

JP and I were in the same dunces group, Class Thirteen. We became friends. Our Irish teacher Father Brady did not even attempt to give poor JP even the rudiments of Gaelic. The shy, red-headed youngster was banished to the back of the class with the 'teach yourself Gaelic' (Buntús Cainte) column from that day's *Irish Independent*.

And as a confused boarder, his first week residing in the prison-like junior dormitory was marred by a group of bigger boys kicking in the door of the bathroom cubicle where the pyjama-clad Breen was squatting on the throne. Terrified, he jumped up, pulled his pyjamas about his crotch and promptly shat himself. From then until his unhappy exit five years later, he was known as Chocolate Arse.

So this was my crucible of learning from 1965–70. St Pat's was still essentially a seminar, the nursery for future priests who went on to Maynooth, ordination and a lifetime of smoking fags, drinking Jameson and fly-fishing or golf. Us novices soon learned that the discovery of a possible vocation to the priesthood meant preferential treatment from the soutane-wearing priest teachers.

In the run-up to the Leaving Certificate I was given an option by my father: get a job as a messenger boy with Black's the butcher or become a boarder at St Pat's. I opted for the latter. Religion loomed large in the life of St Pat's. A 6 a.m. bell summoned us to morning Mass (we had two on Sunday). Benediction was nightly. Confessions were compulsory.

This was despite the virtual absence of decent sinning opportunities in or out of the classroom. Seventeen-year-old boys in the all-male institution couldn't get up to much sinning in the Dickensian school buildings or adjoining dairy farm.

Father McGovern was given the short straw. He was obliged to listen to our confessions in an alcove of the surprisingly handsome nineteenth-century chapel attached to the school. His Saturday afternoons were blighted with our monotonous accounts of masturbation. But we made it worse for the poor man.

We devised a cruel game. The pupil who invented the worst sin, and was burdened with the most penance, was the winner. On the first, and sadly last, implementation of the prank, I emerged victorious (jumbo decades of the Rosary coupled with hours of solitary prayer after supper). I had confessed to harbouring sexual feelings for one of the college cows munching grass behind the handball alleys.

The fantastic admission prompted an all-points bulletin, red-alert sermon from the college president, the saintly Father Terry McManus. He mounted the pulpit after our second Sunday Mass (also compulsory) to pontificate on the dangers of sexual confusion among female-starved teenage boys at the all-male school. Most of the younger pupils were baffled by his warning about bestiality.

Recently, John Cornwell comprehensively indicted the sacrament in his new book, *The Dark Box: A Secret History of Confession*. Cornwell laid the blame for the global scandal of paedophile priests – and by implication the destruction of the Catholic Church in Ireland – on confession.

My Protestant friends from childhood were baffled by my weekly trips to Cavan Cathedral to join my classmates for confession. Before Piux X, Catholics' confession was similar to Protestants'. You told God privately of your misdemeanours and asked forgiveness. You did not share them with a priest, who might reek of drink or, worse, see the confessional as a pulling parlour for sex with under-age boys and girls.

There is no doubt that the Roman Catholic Church exerts an everlasting power on its members. Almost into my teens I believed that confessing my sins to a priest cleansed my soul. Leaving Cavan Cathedral after weekly confessions I felt no fear that a fatal tap from my neighbour John McGinnity's Morris Oxford would trigger my immediate ascent heav-enwards to join my two grannies in paradise.

My departure from St Pat's with a mediocre Leaving Cert in 1970 qualified me for nothing more than the mail boat from Dun Laoghaire to Holyhead. Fortunately my father, as deputy editor of the local paper *The Anglo-Celt*, wangled me an apprenticeship of sorts.

During school holidays I had been hired at £3 a week to help the newspaper photographer. I would stand with my sturdy Rolleiflex alongside the goal at Breffni Park, Cavan, the Mecca of Gaelic football, and snap away.

Mercifully, the monochrome frames were large

enough to embrace some printable action every week. At one match I was standing in the goalmouth of a rain-swept Breffni Park on a Sunday afternoon with only a gaggle of supporters sitting on the grim concrete seats as I peered into the viewfinder at a collection of mud-encrusted players skidding and sliding across the pitch.

Just before half time, a bald man in an overcoat approached me. From his lapel fluttered, on a piece of string, a square of cardboard the size of a paperback book. Emblazoned on the card was the word Steward. 'Who would you be?' he asked. I explained that I was the photographer from *The Anglo-Celt*. Despite the fact that in a small town he already knew who I was, he looked me up and down. 'Do you have any identificay-shun?' he asked.

I replied in the negative. Pulling himself up to his full height, he declared, 'Well, I'm afraid you'll have to leave.' Hands behind his back, feet together military-style, he looked up at the sky. In desperation, I blurted out that my father was Andy McEntee and my late grandfather Andy McEntee had been one of the founders of the GAA in County Cavan.

He looked me up and down. 'So, you're one of the McEntees? Well, all right, you can stay, but next time you have to bring some identificayshun. You see, we have a problem with Yankees and such like coming over here with their cameras and filming the matches and selling the film. We have to be careful.'

As he spoke, I looked at the forlorn dozen or so die-hard supporters of Cornafean and Mullahoran shivering in the rain as they watched their teams play in a match of no consequence on a bleak Sunday afternoon.

My new job as trainee reporter included attendance at Gregg shorthand classes at the local technical school. My incarceration as a boarder had denied me the social equipment to deal with the all-girl class. They were delightful, precocious sixteen-year-olds acquiring office skills. They were much more sophisticated than me. They laughed a lot, mostly at the gauche, pimpled boy in their midst struggling to get up to sixty words a minute.

Soon I had acquired a serious girlfriend. I'd met her on a charity walk from her native Belturbet via Milltown. She was Colette Fitzpatrick, the very attractive daughter of a saintly farming couple, Phil and Kitty Fitzpatrick of Putighan. We subsequently married and enjoyed a tre-mendously happy twenty-five years together. We share two wonderful sons and a delightful daughter. Our subsequent sad divorce was entirely my fault, down to selfishness, drink and sex. But I leap forward too hastily.

Walking the ten miles home from my girlfriend's

farmhouse at 2 a.m., I would enter into futile pacts with my dead grannies to get a lift home. There were few cars on the road at that time and the headlights of an approaching vehicle could be discerned a mile off. I would declare, 'Granny McEntee and Granny Cusack, if you can get this car to stop and give me a lift home I will get you out of purgatory.' This celestial furnace was, and remains, the purging factory for heaven.

The amount of time spent in purgatory is laughingly measured in years, and I had memorised a number of prayers from memoriam cards, which offered time off for prisoners in purgatory – like a sort of celestial Nectar card.

For example, incanting, 'In the name of the Father and the Son and the Holy Ghost' wiped seven years off a granny's sentence. Deal done, the car stops and I forget all about my pledge. If it passed, I would shake my fist at the night sky warning the grannies they must do better. They never did.

At least they weren't in the adjoining B&B, Limbo. This was for Protestants and Roman Catholic babies who had died before baptism. In my infant school, one of the Poor Clare nuns set us a dilemma. If you are holding a dying unbaptised baby, do you (a) summon medical help or (b) find a water tap and carry out an emergency christening?

The answer was always (b). The first time, I gave the

wrong answer and received a rap on the knuckles from Sister's ruler. I was four years old.

Now the church has abolished Limbo and I always annoy my saintly priest cousin Father Johnny Cusack by asking what happened to its residents. Did they get a free transfer to heaven or are they languishing in the flames of purgatory with their baptised kinsfolk?

Both of my parents were devout, kneeling each night by their double bed saying their prayers. Though my father's Roman Catholic compassion did not extend to his younger brother Kevin, a drunk who had fled to England after allegedly drinking out the family bar and grocery business located at the butt of Cavan's half-acre no-go area (tinkers, alcoholic ex-British soldiers and chancers). Kevin was the black sheep of the family. He was never spoken of. In my babyhood, he had departed to London in disgrace.

His widowed mother, my granny, pined for her youngest son, even answering newspaper advertisements for cleaners in the British capital. In her seventies, she naively believed that London was only slightly larger than Cavan and a few discreet enquiries after Mass would establish Kevin's whereabouts. He had compounded his shame by marrying Kathleen, a woman ten years older who had endured the misfortune of having two daughters out of wedlock – not by Kevin – who were lovingly described by my uncle as 'my nieces'.

Resembling the short, fat one in Abbott and Costello, Kevin was a delightful drunk, haunted by his failure to keep in touch with his aged mother until her death in the late '60s. My father never spoke of him and even my attempts at reconciliation with his youngest sibling before his death in 1997 were only partially successful.

Arriving in London in 1975, I barely knew of the existence of Kevin. I subsequently learned that his greatest offence was marrying Kathleen. When I discovered the truth about the background and upbringing of these two mystery cousins who didn't officially exist, I was truly ashamed of my native country.

The Ireland these two illegitimate girls were born into in the late '40s and early '50s was ugly, nasty, mean, vindictive and spiteful.

And it wasn't the landscape that was toxic. It was the people of de Valera's republic: Catholic, but not Christian.

Kathleen, as a naive and gauche young housekeeper to a prosperous farming family, had been raped by the man of the house. She became pregnant. The shame was life-changing. She had the baby. She left her in the care of her spinster sister in a remote farmhouse near Virginia, County Cavan.

She became a wards maid at a local hospital, where she met my alcoholic but charming Uncle Kevin. He was in his twenties; she was in her thirties. They saw each other on and off. Kevin was more interested in Powers Gold Label than sex, but Kathleen became pregnant again by another man. Whether by consent or otherwise, I do not know.

This time her baby daughter fetched up at the orphanage run by the Poor Clare nuns in Cavan on the same street where I lived as a child.

Kathleen emigrated to London. On the collapse of the family business, Kevin bolted in shame to the British capital. He renewed his acquaintance with his old girlfriend and they subsequently married.

Eventually the girls were sent for and boarded the Dun Laoghaire ferry and the boat train to Euston. They joined their mother and her new husband in a council flat in east London.

Kevin loved the girls. It was to this scenario I arrived in Fleet Street as a young reporter. Shortly afterwards, my cousin Frankie, newly demobbed from the RAF, took me to visit Kevin and his wife. I had never met my aunt. Our first meeting was commemorated with her tears and a tsunami of holy water sprinkled on Frankie and I.

She was to spend the rest of her life on her knees, not

only as a cleaner, but mainly begging God for forgiveness for her so-called youthful promiscuity.

But who were the two pretty women sitting demurely on the sofa sipping tea in the cramped front room of Kevin's high-rise apartment?

The youngest – then aged about twenty-five – declared matter-of-factly, 'You don't know me but I know you. When I was in the orphanage in Cavan I used to look out through the gates onto the street and see you holding your mother's hand as she pushed the pram with your baby brother inside.' She knew our names and background. I didn't know she existed.

But my parents did know about the nieces. So did my uncles and aunts. Apart from my saintly Aunt Anna, the family shunned Kevin. So much so that when he arrived in Cavan on holiday with his wife in the '70s, his older brother and his spouse refused to open the door when they called. The older girl also knew my history. She spoke of her ordeal as a pupil in the local primary school near Virginia.

She recalled:

> Once the teacher set us an essay in class to write about our fathers. I didn't know who my father was so I made it up. When we finished she sat at her desk reading them. Then she summoned me to the front of the class.

> She said loudly, 'This girl is a liar. She hasn't got a father
> yet she has written this essay about him. A liar.'

One of the girls married successfully and is now a grandmother. The other has been less fortunate and has dropped from view. The older one contacted me recently to ask advice about exhuming the body of the dead farmer she believes to be her natural father. She would like a DNA test to prove his paternity. I advised her against such a move on the basis that it wouldn't just be a coffin that was opened.

Has Ireland changed? I hope so, but in modern Germany they like to think no one was a member of the Nazi Party. In modern France, no one, apparently, collaborated with the Germans. In 21st-century Ireland, still top-heavy with Catholics but few Christians, no one ostracised my Uncle Kevin and his penitent wife, and in modern Ireland no one was unkind to my mystery cousins, Kevin's 'lovely nieces'.

Kevin's wife Kathleen did her best to keep him sober. Sprinkling holy water on him, her mantra was: 'The devil grips you, Kevin, when you drink.'

Having met him and his family, my next encounter was a telephone call from a payphone in the London Hospital, Whitechapel. He was having his varicose veins

treated and was lonely. I went to see him. He sat, a raincoat over his pyjamas, on the edge of his bed and pointed
to a bedside locker. 'Open that,' he commanded.

Inside, two rows of cans of Long Life, a popular ale
at the time, filled the locker. Kevin drank two. I had
one. At the conclusion of my visit, he offered to walk
me to the front door of the Dickensian hospital two
floors below. At the doorway I bade him farewell and
turned right for the nearby Tube. Kevin didn't turn back
and re-enter the hospital. I watched as he dodged traffic, his raincoat flapping, crossed the street and went
into a pub. He was at the hospital for two weeks, much
of the time spent in the alehouse. Eventually, an off-
duty nurse with her boyfriend spotted the raincoat-clad
figure spouting at the bar. His face was familiar. Then
the pyjamas settled the matter. It was one of her patients,
Kevin McEntee.

Kathleen would have been appalled. She certainly prolonged his life by a few years. But as he lay in his final
coma in a curtained bed in a bleak ward at Whipp's
Cross Hospital in east London, I was summoned to say
farewell. Doing well in Fleet Street, I had commissioned
Sligo tailor Joseph Martin to measure me for my first
Savile Row suit – a Prince of Wales check with, fortu-
itously as it emerged, a spare pair of trews.

I arrived by minicab to the dingy hospital equipped with a carrier bag of brandy miniatures. It was to be a long night. Kevin was in his final coma, sleeping fitfully. I sat by the bed talking to him and placing between his lips the open top of the first brandy miniature. His lips pit-patted together in silent satisfaction. It was a process that continued until his death at 4 a.m.

Leaving the bedside, I called my minicab driver on my mobile and asked him to pick me up at the side entrance he had decanted me at eight hours before. Walking down the dimly lit ground-floor corridor, I found the door locked. I peered out through the 4 x 2 ft glass opening, where a pane of glass had been shattered, and spotted the car and driver. 'Can you go around to the main entrance and I'll meet you there?' I asked. He shook his head in the negative. 'It's a one-way system. I'll have to go out and back in. Can't you climb through the window?'

I spotted a discarded supermarket trolley parked beside a broken seat in the corridor and wheeled it over to the bolted door. Clambering in, I thrust my right leg out of the window. Half in and half out, the trolley starting to move away from me. Two nurses going off duty walked past outside and I asked them for help in exiting the hospital.

They giggled but gamely complied. As they grabbed my arms and heaved, the material in the left posterior section of my lovely, new, bespoke Prince of Wales check suit caught in a shard of remaining glass at the bottom of the window frame.

As they made a final heave there was a loud ripping noise as my expensive trouser leg split in two from arse to ankle, inflicting a long, thin, superficial cut to my leg. On the pavement, my ravaged trouser leg flapping like a rogue sail and blood dribbling over my sock, I waved my fist at the sky. 'Fuck you, Kevin. Is this the thanks I get?' The nurses and the driver unsuccessfully stifled laughter.

Kevin and my uncle Mickey were so different they could have been born on separate planets. When I landed a job with the *Irish Press* in Dublin in 1972, Mickey, my mother's older brother, was furious. He loathed the *Irish Press* and its proprietor Éamon de Valera. Mickey, a well-nourished figure in a three-piece suit, billiard-ball bald, teetotal and the father of eight children, was placid and even-tempered until the subject of politics came up. He hated Éamon 'Long String of Misery' de Valera with a passion. Mickey, a staunch pro-Treaty Fine Gaeler remembered Dev's opposition to the Treaty and Fianna Fáil's subsequent refusal to cooperate, triggering the civil war.

Mickey was election agent for the former Blueshirts in Cavan. Fine Gael Member of Parliament Tom Fitzpatrick was his protégé. Post-Treaty antagonism between Mickey's Fine Gael and Dev's Fianna Fáil was still running high fifty years after the civil war.

Election counts were then held at Cavan Courthouse, a five-minute walk from the McEntee family home in Church Street.

Mickey's habit during counts was to adjourn to our kitchen for refreshment and listen on the radio to the national results streaming in to RTÉ from Dublin.

On this occasion in the mid-'60s, Fine Gael was losing badly to the loathed Fianna Fáil and Mickey, ear glued to the receiver, was in a foul mood.

At least five of my mother's seven children were huddled over lunch at the adjoining table when my sainted mater broke the news of the sudden death of our next-door neighbour Garda Bill Gaffey during the previous night. Gaffey was almost as passionate about Fine Gael as Mickey.

'Poor Guard Gaffey didn't vote this election,' ventured my mother. Mickey's reaction was instantaneous. His face reddened as he stood up and barked, 'That's the dirty shite. 'Tis his civic duty to vote!' Aged about twelve, I, in tandem with my younger brothers and sisters, dropped our knives and forks in shock at the sound and fury. Language like this was not used in the McEntee household. Quickly my mother explained that Gaffey had died. With a lightning execution of the shortened version of the sign of the cross, Mickey exclaimed, 'May the Lord have mercy on his soul.'

Thus Mickey's annoyance at my *Irish Press* job. The *Irish Independent* certainly. Even the Protestant *Irish Times* at a pinch. But the *Press*! I was a turncoat. How could I betray the tradition of the Cusacks of Lavey, who had been staunch Fine Gaelers since the party's formation? From then, to Mickey, I was a lost cause.

I didn't care. I was leapfrogging from compiling the local news notes for Arva and Killeshandra for *The Anglo-Celt* to the Big Smoke. At the age of nineteen, I was off to Dublin and £18 a week on the daily, evening and Sunday titles housed in Burgh Quay.

PART 2

DUBLIN

I already had a girlfriend who had migrated to the civil service in Dublin. In an unsuccessful, earlier bid to join her, I had lobbied the late Bill Shine at the *Irish Independent* for a job. Bill kindly sat me in the newsroom in Middle Abbey Street and asked me to type out a report of a fire that had occurred that day in Dublin. After reading my painstakingly compiled, error-strewn bulletin, Bill kindly pointed out that the last paragraph should have been the intro and bade me good luck. Across in the *Irish Times* office in Fleet Street, a very well-refreshed post-luncheon news editor Donal Foley introduced me to staff: 'Rosemary is from Killeshandra, Joe is from Cootehill and our religious affairs correspondent used to work for the *Celt*. Cheerio.'

Charles Dickens would have been proud to conjure some of the characters that inhabited the lost world of the *Irish Press* newsroom on Burgh Quay.

Among them, Bill Redmond, the patrician chief news editor. Or Paddy 'Much Blood' Clare, the Nighttown reporter who had fought for the IRA in 1916. Or Major Vivion de Valera, with his foolish dream of creating a black, tinted-glass media centre modelled on the *Daily Express* in Fleet Street.

Dublin then was only marginally less ugly than it is now. Behind the *Irish Press* plant on Burgh Quay, on a site once graced by the Theatre Royal, the Stalinist Hawkins House loomed over the neighbourhood. Across the Liffey was the Irish Free State's answer to a skyscraper, Liberty Hall, which blighted the river view. Fianna Fáil was pulling down Georgian Dublin. Shortly after my departure to London, they destroyed Viking Dublin too.

A bedsit no larger than four telephone kiosks in Rathmines was mine for about £5 a week. Smithwick's was about fifteen pence a pint and the No. 12 bus took me all the way to Westmoreland Street, a few minutes' walk from the *Irish Press* HQ.

The front office, open to the public, was adorned with a row of attractive girls acting as receptionists and selling advertisements to those who walked in off the street.

I was soon to learn that this was also where junior reporters spent a depressingly large amount of their time, dispatched by the news editor upstairs to deal with cranks, bums and the deranged.

One colleague, Des Nix, was sent down to placate a nutty old lady clutching a large, faux leather bag with multicoloured patches. She asked Des to turn around as she had something to show him. Des turned to face the bank of female receptionists. The mad woman produced a bull whip and proceeded to lash Des on the back as she ranted incoherently.

On my first day, I trudged up the wooden stairs to be greeted by ruddy-faced northerner Mick O'Kane, the assistant chief news editor, soon to replace Bill Redmond as boss. Redmond was a dead ringer for Marlon Brando in *Apocalypse Now*, only with hair. He sat as a brooding presence amid the mêlée of a smoke-filled newsroom festooned with Underwood typewriters, full ashtrays and wires dangling from the ceiling connected to a profusion of black Bakelite telephones on the large tables that filled the first-floor room overlooking the River Liffey.

Reporters, all puffing on cigarettes, sat noisily clattering out stories on the battered typewriters. Copy paper, carbons, metal spikes and notebooks lay scattered on every surface.

In a series of door-less cubicles located alongside the news desk, female copytakers with earphones feverishly typed copy from the courts, the Dáil and provincial centres. Behind the closed door of the wire room, ticker tape vomited copy from abroad.

Redmond sat Buddha-like at the table that dissected the room, separating the reporters from the sub-editors. Alongside him was O'Kane and the *Evening Press* news editor Dermot MacIntyre and his deputy Mick O'Toole. Behind them – never sitting, always pacing – was Sean Ward, the angst-ridden editor of the *Evening Press*. Redmond was a patrician figure who ruled the newsroom like a disciplinarian headmaster. Because of his girth he was cruelly called Bucklebelly, but generally he meant well towards me and wasn't vindictive.

Sporadic scaffolding and builders wandering between the desks in overalls confirmed Major Dev's grand scheme to create Dublin's answer to Fleet Street's Black Lubyanka.

I was not long in situ when the dust and dirt caused by the construction prompted the NUJ to insist on regular air breaks for staff. Every two hours into a shift there was a mass exodus from the editorial floor into Burgh Quay for fifteen-minute respites.

Some inhaled the dank, hop-scented air on the banks of the Liffey river, which meandered past the office.

Others disappeared into the White Horse, Silver Swan and other pubs, which opened early for dockers.

I can still conjure up an image of NUJ militant Mick Cronin leading the charge street-wards. The first air break of the morning.

The NUJ action was my first taste of the epic industrial strife that was to contribute hugely to the final demise of the *Irish Press* in 1994.

On that first morning, myself and a fellow rookie, Michael Sharkey from Derry, were led by Mick O'Kane to a dank cubby hole described as Daytown, where a radio receiver was tuned to the frequency used by the city's Garda Síochána. Mick told us to alert him to any breaking stories on the police frequency.

For hours, Sharkey and I sat on full alert, our ears tuned to the staccato barking of Garda. 'Delta One, Delta One, stolen car located in Talbot Street, number O Oscar, Z for Zebra, U for Under...' Wow, this was the cutting edge. Weaned on farmer's meetings and family land disputes at Bailieborough Circuit Court, I was now in the big time, listening to dramas from the mean streets of the Big D.

Mick and I competed to get O'Kane's attention, rushing to his desk and bringing details of vagrants, minor accidents and inconsequential shop lifting. 'Well done, lads,' he recited mantra-like, his attention on other matters. 'Keep your ears open.'

Sharkey, who was slightly younger than I and as a result was paid only £17 a week, suggested we find a small flat together. We found a furnished hovel in Rathgar Road with two fold-down sofas that doubled as beds. Sharkey soon realised our new abode was only a few streets away from the Dublin home of then Taoiseach Jack Lynch.

Both of us had a day off when some neighbours of Mick's from Derry came for tea. A school contemporary of Mick's had just appeared in the newly created Special Criminal Court on firearms charges. His mother and father, along with assorted cousins and friends, had come up to Dublin to visit him in Mountjoy Prison.

'I'm sure if we wrote to Jack Lynch he'd do something for our wee boy,' ventured the mother. Mick mischievously advised her that Jack lived not five minutes away.

'Oh, we must go and ask him to help our wee boy,' declared the mother, already on her feet.

Mick, confident that we wouldn't get past the Lynch Garda security detail, led the way across Rathgar Road and on to the Lynch home. An open gate led into a sweeping gravel driveway. To the right of the gate was a hut that should have contained at least one member of the Garda Síochána. It didn't.

It was empty. Nervously, Mick and I scrunched up the drive with our party of Derry Nationalists. We looked left and right in search of Garda machine guns, revolvers, batons. Nothing.

We got to the front door and the prisoner's mother rang the bell. Almost immediately it was opened by Jack's wife Maureen, wearing a dressing gown with a towel wrapped around her head. Looking startled, she asked who we were.

Missus Derry burst into tears and launched into a rambling rant about her innocent boy being wrongly locked up in Mountjoy. Instinctively, Maureen Lynch stepped forward and embraced the weeping woman. Just then, a red-faced Garda, his dishevelled trousers suggesting he might have been answering a call of nature, scrunched into view and grabbed the woman. Mrs Lynch's reaction was immediate. 'Please, Garda. I am speaking to this lady.' The policeman, no doubt imagining his imminent transfer to the Aran Islands, stepped back.

With commendable panache, Maureen Lynch explained that her husband was at the Dáil, but if Missus Derry would care to write a note, she would see that her husband received it. Pen and paper were provided, a note written and handed to Mrs Lynch. We departed.

A few weeks later, the felon's mother received a

personal reply from Jack Lynch explaining that her son's future was in the hands of the court. Class or what?

Soon after joining the paper I heard the story of Redmond summoning a copy boy (we still had them then) and proffering a £20 note. 'Get me twenty singles,' boomed Bill. Off the lad went into Burgh Quay, returning half an hour later with a steaming parcel. 'What's that?' asked Redmond 'Twenty singles, and here's your change' replied the copy boy. He had interpreted the order in the Dublin lingo of a single meaning a solitary bag of chips. He had bought Redmond twenty bags!

Not long after joining the *Press*, I was awarded my first freebie. It was clearly a junket that no one more experienced on the paper would have touched with a barge pole. Here is how Mick O'Kane phrased it: 'Do you fancy a trip to Liverpool? Your first overseas assignment.' The ferry company B&I was launching a new roll on/roll off facility on the Mersey and a journalist from each paper had been invited to sail on the eight-hour trip on the *Leinster*, reporting on the event and returning by sea. 'Yes, please,' I replied.

The outward trip was a blur of alcohol in the company of B&I's Keith Gronbach and other seasoned topers. I can't remember any details of Liverpool or the event, but the return trip to the North Wall was memorable.

In the bar of the ship I got into a conversation with an extremely well-nourished female street vendor from Dublin's Moore Street Market on her way back from buying merchandise in Liverpool. She was probably in her early thirties but I thought she was ancient. It didn't matter.

Her mission was to purchase a wholesale consignment of a small plastic male doll mounted on a podium that was filled with water. Called Cheeky Charlie, when his plastic trousers were pulled down, he peed like a water pistol. After much non-intellectual conversation fuelled by Guinness and Cork Dry Gin, Cheeky John adjourned at 3 a.m. with the well-lubricated female to the deserted upper-deck lounge of the good ship *Leinster*.

Frantic fumbling and slobbering kisses were followed by the most unromantic congress imaginable. The whole sorry business took no more than four minutes and was serenaded by some stunning seagull farts (male and female). Cheerio then, Bridie, or whoever, I thought. We'll never meet again. I was wrong.

Weeks later, while strolling down Dublin's Henry Street (adjacent to the Moore Street Market) on a sunny Saturday afternoon, hand in hand with my girlfriend, all seemed right with the world. Passing the entrance to Moore Street, a roly-poly female vendor was bellowing, 'Get your Cheeky Charlies! Get your Cheeky Charlies!'

I failed to recognise her. Unfortunately, the same could not be said for her. Suddenly she started to wave in my direction. 'Howya, John? How's it going?'

Then the penny dropped. I'd never seen her in daylight (even in the dark she was no head-turner), but I recognised her. I ignored her greeting and urged my precious petal to accelerate. She noticed the old slapper bellowing in my direction. 'She's waving at you, John. She knows you.'

I insisted she was mistaken, that she was a demented harridan from the market: 'Ignore her, dear, let's move along,' I pleaded.

My thwarted and furious Moore Street squeeze got the message and immediately changed tack. With an outburst that could be heard in O'Connell Street, she roared, 'Jasus, John, you weren't so fucking shy when you were riding me on the *Leinster*!'

To paraphrase Philip Larkin, sex was in its infancy in Dublin in the early '70s – though I did have my moments. In one of the numerous flats I shared with Sharkey, I had to entertain his thirty-something aunt who was on a trip from her home in Liverpool. Sharkey was detained on a late shift.

Married with a young family, she seemed elderly to someone who was not yet twenty. We went on a drinking spree in O'Connell Street fuelled by a ten-pound

note she had kindly proffered. In those days, after closing time you queued endlessly on St Stephen's Green for
rare taxis. On our way to Rathgar, we had a snog and a
fumble, followed by full-blown sex up against the boiler
in a shed at the back of our bedsit. Romantic or what?

My longest stint in Dublin's flatland was in 1974–75, in
the top half of a magnificent red-stoned villa on Palmerston
Road, opposite the home of Dr Garret FitzGerald. Apart
from myself and Mick Sharkey, there were three others:
Seamus and Pat, two trainee managers at Woolworths,
and Pajo, a car mechanic with literary pretensions.

Sharkey inexplicably moved out when I offered bed
space to a fellow colleague Alan Murray, a journalist
from Belfast who was hired by the *Irish Press* in 1973.
He happened to be a Protestant from Belfast's Ravenhill
Road, haunt of the notorious Shankill Butchers.

It took me some weeks to discover that Sharkey could
not bear to share the same house as Murray. Sharkey's
family were Nationalist Catholics from Derry; the
Murrays were Loyalist Protestants from east Belfast.

I had the privilege of staying in both the Sharkey and
Murray homes on opposite sides of the sectarian divide.
Apart from the picture of the Pope in one house and the
Queen in the other, there was little difference in the *Coro-
nation Street*-type dwellings occupied by both families.

Driving to Belfast with Alan Murray on our way to a package holiday in Spain (it was cheaper to fly out of Belfast than Dublin), he uttered a word of caution as we approached his family home in east Belfast. The so-called Shankill Butchers, a gang of murderers intent on torturing and killing Catholics, was at the height of its notoriety.

'If we are stopped', warned Alan, 'say your religion is Plymouth Brethren.' 'Why Plymouth Brethren?' I asked. 'Because it is the only religion they don't understand,' Murray replied.

Alan's mother was ironing in the small kitchen when we arrived. I was shown the small door leading to the stairs and the attic. If there was an unexpected knock on the door, I was to go straight to the attic. I was too young and naive to be frightened by the implication.

I remember Bruce Forsyth's *The Generation Game* was on the TV as the first of a succession of knocks came to the front door. I was ushered upstairs on each occasion. Each time I was summoned back down to meet a neighbour who had come to borrow sugar/milk/bread/washing powder. Word had spread that a Taig (a Roman Catholic) was staying with the Murrays. None of them had ever met a Catholic. In that small kitchen I was examined and walked around like a sculpture in the Tate Modern.

I remember Mrs Murray, who had two children, Alan and Ian, expressed exasperation when I told her my mother had seven children and two miscarriages. 'Youse Catholics...' she sighed.

More than twenty years later, while working at the *Express*, the show business editor was a likeable Belfast man called John Lyttle. His father had been Tommy Lyttle, leader of the Shankill Butchers and subsequently murdered by an offshoot of his own gang of psychopaths.

John told me that as a twelve-year-old he remembered his father returning home one evening to their east Belfast terraced house and hanging his jacket on the back of the sitting-room door. When young John heard the trill of an approaching ice cream van on the street, he asked his dad for some money to buy a 99p cone. The father beckoned to his jacket. 'I put my hand in the jacket pocket to get some money,' John recalled, 'and I found a human finger.'

Alan brought Protestant precision to our otherwise chaotic Dublin flat. Some dormant spirit of non-sectarianism prompted us to award Alan the prize bedroom, with its single bed and maximum privacy on the first floor of the human zoo that was Palmerston Road.

A week after his arrival, he and I returned from a 3–11 p.m. shift to find fellow reporter Brendan Burke sitting on the sofa, his hands bandaged – one of them clutching a bottle of Harp Lager.

Brendan, a true Dubliner, lived at home with his parents in Ballyfermot. He had asked if he could bring his fiancée Nonie to our flat while we were at work (the other residents had gone home for the weekend).

His plan was to have her fry some chips with our deep-fat fryer and then enjoy some illicit coupling in the empty love nest. Unfortunately, the chipper erupted in flames and Nonie suffered severe burns to her hands and arms. Brendan called an ambulance and ungallantly decided to remain in the flat while Nonie was taken off to hospital.

Brendan stayed drinking bottles of Harp from a pile of six-packs he had brought for his romantic evening. I went to bed. Unbeknownst to me, Brendan had hopped into bed beside Alan Murray.

Alan and I were on the 8 a.m. *Evening Press* shift the following morning and on the drive to work Alan was silent. After the initial rush of rewriting and phone calls, Alan asked, 'Can I have a word? How well do you know Burke?'

I explained that he was a close friend and I had known him since my first day in Dublin more than two years before. 'Why do you ask?' I said.

Looking at the floor, Alan, all of 5 ft 2 in., explained

that after Brendan had clambered in beside him at 2 a.m., he had declared, 'I miss Nonie. Do you mind if I have a wank?' Before Alan could respond, Brendan proceeded to agitate his member at high speed, causing the small bed to vibrate and shudder. Alan clutched the blankets, holding on for dear life until Brendan, mercifully after a short time, ejaculated and declared, 'That's better', before promptly falling into a deep, snore-laden sleep. Alan didn't know what had hit him. Nothing like that had ever happened to him before. So different from his home life on Belfast's Ravenhill Road.

Shortly afterwards, Brendan brought Nonie on a trip to my native Cavan. As was the convention, he stayed with me in the family home in Church Street. Nonie stayed with my soon-to-be wife Colette in Putighan, near Belturbet, ten miles away. My mother liked Brendan a lot. In my hire-purchase white Ford Cortina we motored to the small village of Milltown to visit the ancient Drumlane Abbey.

Milltown was the home of a local country and western star called Ian Corrigan. His mother ran the village grocery/post office. Brendan offered to get ice cream, which in that pre-Magnum era was cut from a block according to size and cost.

Brendan ordered and paid for the biggest wafers but

returned to the car with the measliest ice creams imaginable. I asked who had served him. He replied, 'The woman started cutting the ice cream and I noticed this poster of a big bollix on the wall behind her. I pointed at it and said, "Who the fuck is Ian Corrigan?"' It was her son.

At the conclusion of that trip, Brendan and I were in Geoghan's Bar on Church Street when I complained about having to return to Dublin for my 3–11 p.m. shift (Brendan was on the same rota). 'I'm going sick, why don't you get a sick cert?'

I'd already had two pints of Guinness when I headed for Dr Con Linehan's surgery in nearby Farnham Street. 'I'm not well,' I explained. He looked at me suspiciously. 'What do you mean you are not well?' I replied, 'I'm run down.'

My complexion, glowing with a quarter of a gallon of Guinness, told a different tale. Dr Linehan ordered me to drop my trousers and administered a vitamin injection. I gave him the then normal payment of one pound in return for a sick note and trotted down the steps of his Georgian-terraced surgery, across Ashe Street towards Geoghan's. By the time I rejoined Brendan at the bar I really did feel ill and had to go home and lie down. Thanks, Dr Linehan.

Sadly, Brendan was taken from us as he crossed the road in Ballyfermot and was struck by a car. He'd married

Nonie and had two lovely children and just wasn't quick enough to avoid the speeding car.

One of the reasons he wasn't as fast on his feet was that, a few years before, he had wrapped his car around a pole near the Guinness Brewery. Brendan had been catching the eye of the barman in Mulligan's in Poolbeg Street all evening and was more than well refreshed.

The *Irish Press* news desk secretary Miss Betty called me in London to explain that Brendan had had to be cut out of his destroyed vehicle. She said, 'Thank God Brendan had had a few drinks. He was relaxed. If he'd been sober he'd have been killed.'

My flatmate Seamus, a trainee manager in Woolworths, had an enviable and astonishing success rate with the ladies. Women, who were invariably gorgeous, were attracted to Seamus. We shared a bedroom and he would sit up in bed at night rehearsing songs like 'Canadian Pacific' and 'The German Clockwinder' for forthcoming weddings. He was an awful singer but he had the confidence, panache and charm to get away with grim caterwauling.

Despite his promiscuity, Seamus retained that primitive Irish Catholic belief in good and evil. When his cherished Mini was stolen, he abandoned sex, prayed and went to confession. It was recovered within a week and he was back shagging.

In the glove compartment of the car was a small, glass container of mud. I asked him what it was: 'It's clay from St Mogue's Island on Lough Erne. He is the patron saint of fire prevention and with the clay my car will never go on fire.' It never did.

One bank holiday weekend, Seamus and the other flat-mates had returned to the country and I was lumbered with a 6 p.m.–2 a.m. shift on the *Sunday Press*. The company paid for a taxi home at the ungodly hour of 2 a.m.

I asked the driver to leave me on Rathmines Road so I could buy some chips from an all-night café. As I emerged, I was approached by a looming Gerard Depardieu-like figure, all of 6 ft 4 in. in height. 'Do you know where I could get a bed and breakfast?' he asked in a rural County Limerick accent. I told him to enquire at the local Garda station. He already had.

I knew I had a large empty apartment a quarter of a mile away, but did I want the Incredible Hulk to leap from his bed and throttle me? (Working in newspapers, covering atrocities, sharpens the imagination.)

I decided to let him walk alongside as I thought what I should do. He told me that he was a farmer in County Limerick who had a long-standing relationship with a local girl who worked in the civil service in Dublin and who returned to see him at weekends. Recently she had stopped coming home to visit. Without consulting her, he had decided to come to Dublin and surprise his girl. When he turned up at her address in Rathmines, she was appalled. She wouldn't let him in. 'Through the letter box,' he confided, 'I could hear people laughing at me.' He had been wandering the streets of the strange city since.

I decided to take a chance. 'I have a room if you like,' I said, leading him up the garden path to the front door, and up the stairs to the small attic room usually occupied by Pajo, the car mechanic.

I then went downstairs and found an abandoned mahogany chair leg, which I placed under the bed. I also put a wooden chair under the doorknob to thwart any potential attack.

The following morning I was in a deep sleep when I heard the door knob being rattled. I jumped up, grabbed the chair leg and shouted, 'I'm armed! You can fuck off now!' All I heard was a mumbled 'thank you, I'm going now', followed by the tramp of feet and the front door slamming. I looked at my watch. It was 10 a.m.

Gingerly I removed the chair and peered out into the empty hall. There was no one else in the flat. I climbed the stairs to the attic room and found a large £5 note (at this time a pint of ale was 20p) sitting on the dressing table next to a scrawled note. It said: 'Dear Sir, thank you so much for your kindness in taking me in. I'll not forget you. Please accept this small token of my gratitude... All the best, Tom.'

Soon after my arrival in Dublin, I was a regular in Mulligan's of Poolbeg Street, the ancient and historic pub located a short stroll from the back door of the *Irish Press* building on the next block. In stressful moments I still conjure up the image of Mulligan's circa 1973, pints of perfect Guinness standing sentry-like atop the wooden counter. On the stools at the bar, the one furthest from the back door of the *Irish Press*, sit contentedly a variety of ghosts.

My brother Andy talking non-stop to his friend Gerry McMorrow; Brendan Burke regaling Tom McPhail with his sexual encounter with the assistant librarian; Kieran 'Lust for Glory' Patten telling fellow Scotsman Larry Kilday that everyone but him is an idiot; Mick Cronin spouting amiable gibberish in a language only he understands; and, nursing a globe of brandy mixed with milk, Con Houlihan standing majestically at the bar, his face camouflaged with a raised hand.

Departed now to the celestial saloon, they are all tangible in my head – living, breathing, drinking, talking in the shadow of the newspaper that formed us.

Another haunting day. This time without ghosts. The same bar. Coming up to 2.30 p.m. – the Holy Hour, when

Dublin's pubs closed for an hour, originally to allow apprentice barmen to attend Mass. It was now a device to clear the alehouse of morning drunks and chancers.

I had just finished the Daytown early shift and, entering Mulligan's just before the Holy House closure, was greeted by co-patron Con Cusack from Lavey in County Cavan. He was putting the shutters on the windows and preparing to sweep the floor. He then opened the door of the men's toilet and heaved a bucket of warm water spiced with Jeyes Fluid through the open cavity and feverishly mopped as the liquid lapped the tiled floor.

Pages from a copy of the previous Sabbath's *Sunday Press* torn into neat squares were placed on a string next to the lavatory. I joked with Con that after availing myself of his thunderbox and wiping myself clean with the newspaper I could return to my Rathmines apartment, seek a mirror and read on my buttocks the journalistic genius of *Sunday Press* editor Vincent Jennings. He didn't laugh. He rarely did.

Con poured me a pint of Guinness in the deserted saloon bar. I stared at my solitary, perfect pint, deep black topped by a thick clerical collar of bright beige. Nectar.

In the empty, swept bar, smelling of ale dregs and disinfectant, sunlight filtering through the slats of the shutters, I sipped my Guinness. For that lone illicit hour, in the warm womb of Mulligans, my work done and aged twenty-one, I was in paradise.

One of the perks of working at Burgh Quay as a junior minion was being selected by Gerry Fox, the Brylcreemed, sharp-faced news editor of the *Sunday Press*, to accompany a seasoned photographer on a country run out of Dublin in one of the mandarin-coloured VW Beetles.

We were in search of whimsy, local stories about bizarre achievements, unusual farm animals, local celebrities.

It could be Kerry or Galway or Limerick, but the routine was set in stone: leave Dublin on Monday, stay in a reasonably priced hotel touring the area in search of material and return on Thursday to write up your stories the following day. Gerry Fox was supposed to give us some 'leads', which invariably led nowhere.

Looking back over thirty years, I am still astonished that we were not expected to contact the office while away. In the age before mobile phones, we did not get in touch to say we were staying in so and so. We were incommunicado from the time Dougie Dougan or Sean Larkin pointed the car towards the Naas dual carriageway and the open road.

Once, the late, great snapper Eddie McDonnell and I stayed in Waterford's most exclusive hotel overlooking that wonderful city. We didn't have credit cards and I remember on checking out we had to assemble our available notes and then do cartwheels to achieve a discount.

The night before, Eddie had driven the VW in the direction of a fish-and-chip shop, knowing that we really couldn't afford the dinner rates at our hotel. We returned to the hotel with our vinegar-drenched suppers wrapped in newspaper.

A snooty waiter approached us as we sat in the residents lounge with our pungent plunder. 'Can I help you?' he sniffed. Eddie sent him off to get more salt and vinegar – 'Oh, and a couple of plates, thanks,' he added.

We were surrounded by the members of the local Chamber of Commerce, who looked at us disdainfully over their gin and tonics. Eddie smirked back and then leaned over to say, 'Wait till you see. When they get the smell, they'll be jealous.' The little Dubliner was right. Ten minutes after we tucked in, the Waterford hoi polloi were summoning the jumped-up factotum who had sneered at us and ordering rounds of sandwiches.

Eddie was shameless. Visiting the local MD of a US company that made boots capable of enduring the extreme weather conditions of the north and south poles, he lifted his foot onto the bosses' table, showed a scuffed desert boot, winked and declared, 'I got this sample at another American factory we visited.' He didn't get any free boots.

Photographer Sean Larkin and I visited a tennis ball factory in the Midlands that had just been endorsed by new tennis wunderkid Björn Borg. We'd had some alcoholic refreshments when I approached the receptionist sitting at a desk under two giant tennis balls hanging from the ceiling and asked to speak to the manager. When he appeared, hand outstretched, I declared, 'There a fine big pair of balls you have.' Thank God he was Swedish.

He agreed to allow us to speak to the girls on the production line and for Sean to take some photographs to illustrate the article. Sean almost suffered a cardiac arrest when I asked a group of local ladies of a certain age who were trimming the factory's products, 'How long have you been handling balls?' and 'How many balls a day do you handle?' They weren't Swedish. It was almost impossible to get a complete sentence out of them what with the giggling and tittering.

In the winter of 1974, I was dispatched with photographer Ray Cullen to County Kilkenny to find whimsical stories that might boost local circulation. We'd been told that local resident Jeremiah McCarthy, Ireland's oldest man at 107 years old, had agreed to be the celebratory starter of a forthcoming charity walk in aid of the local Mentally Handicapped Society.

Fuelled by a few lunchtime Guinnesses in Kilkenny,

Ray and I arrived at the McCarthy residence in the picturesque village of Freshford on a biting cold afternoon. We tapped on the half door. It was opened by an elderly lady. 'Are you Mrs Jeremiah McCarthy?' I asked tentatively. She replied, 'No, I'm his daughter.' Ray indiscreetly gave me the thumbs up sign. Blimey, we thought, if this old dear is the daughter, Jeremiah must be as wrinkled as Somerset Maugham.

We were invited into the kitchen for a cup of tea. Jeremiah's daughter explained that he had been confined to bed for the previous two years. He wasn't suffering from any particular ailment, but age had slowed him down. Shamelessly, we pleaded with her to get Jeremiah up and out of bed to be interviewed. At the time, the *Sunday Press* was the largest-selling newspaper in Ireland and the poor dear seemed to feel some obligation to comply with our wishes.

She agreed and disappeared up a slight wooden ramp on the kitchen floor into a corridor concealed behind a door. She was gone for about half an hour. When she returned, she was accompanied by a small, slight figure wearing a starched, grey woollen suit with creases on the trousers sharp enough to shave with.

He clutched a sturdy wooden walking stick in each hand. He was wearing a felt trilby from which strands of white hair peeped out around his ears. His ebony-hued face was adorned with a snow-white drooping moustache. His eyes were bright and alert. He shuffled down the ramp relying on his sticks and slowly made his own way over to a chair beside the kitchen table.

As I greeted him, his daughter explained that he was quite deaf. 'HOW ARE YOU, MR McCARTHY?' I bellowed. He replied quietly, 'I'm fine, thanks be to God.'

What followed was a conversation peppered with my SHOUTED questions and his mouse-like monosyllabic answers. 'TO WHAT DO YOU ATTRIBUTE YOUR GREAT AGE?' I asked. 'Good livin', sleep and whiskey.'

At that stage, whiskey was produced, and his daughter explained that he was a Peace Commissioner and could still sign his name. A pen and paper were produced.

Jeremiah clutched the pen and tried to make contact with the paper. He missed. His shaking hand hovered here, there and everywhere. Eventually his daughter grabbed his wrist and directed him towards the paper. He wrote in a huge meandering scrawl 'Jeremiah McCarthy PC'. We congratulated him like a toddler who has just mastered the art of the chamber pot. More questions followed, but he seemed tired.

My photographer started making frantic gestures and brandishing his cameras. 'Would it be possible', Ray asked, 'to get Jeremiah over to the door so we could get nice shots of him leaning out of the half door?'

Jeremiah's daughter helped him to his feet and he set out on the long, slow, distant journey to the door. When he anchored himself to the bottom half of the door, Ray was already in place outside on the roadway in the sub-zero temperatures. Jeremiah gamely smiled and waved and leaned this way and that. But photographers always require one more and Ireland's oldest man was turning blue by the time Ray decided he'd snapped enough frames. Jeremiah retrieved his sticks and started the interminable shuffle back to the seat at the kitchen table. Half-way there he mumbled something. It was incoherent. 'WHAT WAS THAT, JEREMIAH?' I asked.

He repeated, 'I'd be a long time walking to Dublin.'

When Jeremiah was safely berthed, Ray and I thanked father and daughter and made our exit.

The following weekend, the *Sunday Press* carried a sweet picture of a beaming Jeremiah peering out of his front door. The accompanying story outlined his plans for the charity walk – all fine and dandy. The following day I was walking along O'Connell Street in Dublin en route to a late shift at work when I spotted an even larger picture of Jeremiah on the front page of the *Evening Press*. What's he up to now? I wondered as

I bought a newspaper. The headline said it all: 'Ireland's Oldest Man Dies.'

It transpired that Jeremiah, safely tucked up in bed for two years, had, when obliged to get up and dress to pose in the near-arctic conditions for the *Sunday Press*, caught a fatal chill. He was very swiftly Ireland's former oldest man. To this day I am pointed out by former colleagues as 'The Man Who Killed the Oldest Man in Ireland'. I blame Ray the photographer.

Soon after dispatching Ireland's Oldest Man to a premature grave, I got an unwelcome request from a Northern Irish friend who worked as a cameraman for RTÉ. Could I provide some temporary accommodation for his younger brother Columba, who had got himself into a spot of bother north of the border?

But first, some background. My mother had terrible taste in jumpers and occasionally knitted me presents of garish sweaters that would put a rainbow to shame. One of these, with my name lovingly inscribed on a piece of silk sewn into the neck, was worn only once before its permanent banishment to the back of the wardrobe.

Little did I know it would become useful in dealing with Columba. At the time, Northern Ireland was a cauldron of violence. It was the worst period of the Troubles. Columba McVeigh was a County Tyrone teenager, who, his brother explained, had got himself involved with the IRA and had been picked up and interrogated by the RUC. He was subsequently released and his family wished to get him out of Northern Ireland for fear of further involvement with paramilitaries. Hence the request for a bolthole in Dublin.

I consulted my flatmates and the consensus was that he could stay for a maximum period of one month. A few days later a pimply-faced, shaven-headed, 6 ft 2 in. northerner turned up in jeans, Doc Marten boots, T-shirt and striped lumber shirt clutching a sausage-shaped shoulder bag. 'Where am I kipping?' he asked unsmilingly.

I showed him to a spare bed in the attic bedroom. 'Is there anything to eat?' he enquired after dropping his bag on the bed and shedding his boots. I gestured towards the fridge where he promptly plundered some sausages earmarked by Woolworths' Pat for his evening meal.

'Where's the pan?' he asked as I politely tried to explain that the sausages were not his to fry.

He ignored me, deftly turning on the gas and throwing the entire string of sausages onto the frying pan.

When he brought his feast into the sitting room and plopped down on the sofa in front of the TV, I gingerly tried to explain the fairly primitive house rules. It was obvious he wasn't listening to guidelines about cleaning up afterwards and respecting the food and drink of others.

That first evening was marked by his 'fuck off' response to Pat's demand for an explanation when he returned home and found his sausages were not in the fridge.

He liked to be called Columbo – the TV detective played by Peter Falk. He took control of the TV and when not focused on the screen regaled us with hints at his revolutionary life up north. 'Oh, I could tell you stories,' he boasted. 'I could make the hair on the back of your neck stand up. Oh yeah, I could tell you stories.' These mutterings were accompanied by frequent lifts of his bejeaned hip as he farted long and loud in the general direction of his listeners.

That first evening he eventually retired to bed, leaving his dirty dishes on the floor.

He started as he meant to go on. The weeks with us developed a depressing pattern. Lying in bed until lunchtime, he would rise and scour the fridge, cupboards and bread bin for provisions. He spilt milk everywhere. He discarded crumbs – cereal, bits of egg, sardine, cheese – on his progress from kitchen to sofa. His only trips out were to the newsagent and off-licence. He had also somehow managed to sign on and did collect his dole, though he still borrowed money from most of us. Our evenings were now full of details of his derring-do fight for Irish freedom. He had, of course, shot at least two soldiers, driven a car bomb to a rural police station and was one of the most seasoned and experienced Volunteers of the Irish Republican Army. He had only just celebrated his sixteenth birthday.

The nadir was an evening when we invited some girls back from the pub to the flat. Their arrival distracted Columba from the TV and his six-pack of Smithwick's. He introduced himself.

The girls were wide-eyed with his stories of nocturnal ambushes in the badlands of County Tyrone. He, balaclava-clad, laying waste to Her Majesty's finest troops and the best recruits to the RUC. It was all fantasy and sounded like it. But, in the climate of the time and the atmosphere of unbombed Dublin, Columba never had any shortage of avid listeners.

There was now open hostility between Columba and his reluctant hosts. None of my friends bothered to put any food in the fridge or in the cupboards. His failure to maintain any semblance of tidiness meant that we had all degenerated into a kind of squalor. Hints about leaving had turned into open demands for his departure. Columba would simply throw back his shoulders, square up and say, 'Make me go.' None of us felt able to rise to the challenge.

About six weeks after his arrival, I returned one afternoon from an early Daytown shift on the paper. I found Columba lying on the sofa, clad in an eye-searing multicoloured woollen jumper. I recognised it instantly. It was my mother's discarded gift.

Columba had obviously raided my wardrobe and commandeered the sweater without permission.

I feigned annoyance. It was my favourite jumper, I lied. Then, conscious that he owed me more than £20 and that he had, only that morning, collected his dole, I had a brainwave.

'Tell you what,' I said. 'I'll let you have it for a tenner.'

He eyed me up and then glanced briefly down at the jumper and said, 'It's a deal.'

Miraculously, he handed over the ten pounds. I felt triumphant.

For the three further weeks Columba imposed himself on us as a lodger, the jumper left his back only when he went to bed.

Then, like some insidious dentist's drilling that just suddenly stops, he was gone. No goodbyes. Nothing. He popped out to the newsagents and never came back. We couldn't believe our luck. We waited until the weekend to celebrate.

The following week his older brother called to enquire about his welfare. We told him he'd gone and assumed he'd returned north. By the time I moved to London in 1975, Columba was a distant memory.

It was not until after the Good Friday Agreement and the IRA's permanent ceasefire that I learned the truth. Columba had been set up by the British secret service to find out about IRA border activity. Bullets were planted in his home and he was arrested and taken to Crumlin Road jail to establish his IRA credentials. When he was released, he followed instructions and headed for the home of a local priest suspected of having IRA sympathies. British intelligence wanted to trace the route used by the IRA to spirit wounded volunteers and most wanted out of the jurisdiction to the Irish republic across the nearby border.

The priest was supposed to be at the hub of the escape route. But the reverend father wouldn't let Columba through the front door. Discredited Columba had nowhere to go. He fled to his brother's home in Dublin and eventually landed on us.

After he left our flat in Palmerston Road, the IRA caught up with him. He was bundled into the back of a car and driven away, eventually arriving tied and blindfolded in a remote bog in County Monaghan. There, forced to kneel, Columba was shot in the head and buried in the damp peat. He has lain there undiscovered for more than a quarter of a century, missed only by his family.

When his grave is eventually located as part of the peace process, the Garda Síochána or PFNI will dig him up. He will be wearing the same jumper that accompanied him to his destiny. It is mine, my sainted mother's pride and joy. It is probable that the bog will have even preserved the name tag lovingly sewn into the collar.

Now that I know the truth about Columba, I feel a great sadness for him. He was a pain in the neck, but he was young, at the start of his life, and certainly didn't deserve to have it snuffed out by a bunch of terrorists masquerading as Irish freedom fighters.

Sinn Féin's Gerry Adams persists in vehemently denying that he had anything to do with the similar disappearance and subsequent execution of Belfast woman Jean McConville, who was murdered by the IRA in 1972, allegedly as an informer. This is despite deathbed evidence from one of his IRA colleagues, Brendan Hughes, that Adams ordered the killing when he was a Provisional IRA bigwig in Belfast at the time.

While her body was subsequently found, a new book entitled *Voices from the Grave* provides chapter and verse on Adams's involvement in her killing.

Mrs McConville became one of 'the Disappeared', the unspecified number of Irish men and women executed during the Troubles by the IRA, their bodies secretly buried.

As part of the Anglo-Irish Agreement, the IRA has been identifying the locations of these unmarked graves and giving the still-grieving families a level of closure. Mrs McConville's family have closure. Columba McVeigh's family still waits.

Another sporadic guest at Palmerston Road was my cousin Michael Conlon, who ran a small antiques stall at Dandelion Market in St Stephen's Green. Michael, who went on to great success as an antique dealer, was struggling in 1973. He had been unwell and went home to his father Frank's Killynebber house in Cavan to recuperate. He left his small shop in the care of friend and neighbour Finian Maloney.

When he returned, he found his stock had been sold, with Finian pocketing the takings. He asked to stay as he went in search of Finian in the murky underworld of central Dublin.

He didn't return that night. I was on the Daytown shift the following morning and purchased the City editions of *The Times* and *Independent* at the corner of Hawkins Street on the way to work at 7 a.m.

The front page had accounts of Michael suffering a gunshot wound after he had confronted someone at his shop in St Stephen's Green the previous evening. He was critically ill. I abandoned work and sped to St Vincent's Hospital. I found Michael lucid; the bullet had missed all his vital organs. He had been shot by Finian, but he never told the police. Finian, son of the county surgeon, died later in squalor in London. When a recuperating Michael and I entered Tommy's Bar in Cavan, there was little sympathy. One wag quipped, 'How's Leadbelly?'

Despite the ongoing mayhem in Northern Ireland, it did not impinge on my life in Dublin. It was called Southern Comfort, the total lack of interest of those in the Irish capital to the ongoing civil war a mere hour and a half's drive away.

Working for the pro-Sinn Féin *Irish Press*, we were not allowed to refer to occupied Ulster as Northern Ireland – it was the six counties. A lot of my time between 1972 and 1975 was spent on mindless 3–11 p.m. shifts for the daily broadsheet. We started at 3 p.m. and were obliged to take a break at 5 p.m., returning at 6 p.m. Five interminable hours loomed re-writing copy from the earlier *Evening Press* and extracting boring paragraphs from tedious government ministers' speeches.

Some of the older reporters like Gerry Flanagan, Noel Conway and Michael Barber simply got drunk in Mulligan's, the Swan or the Horse during the break in order to anaesthetise themselves for the evening of re-writes and scripts. Occasionally, very occasionally, a big story broke. Us younger hacks were invariably dispatched to the scene of the drama.

On one memorable night, there was a major riot at Portlaoise Prison. At the time, all the dangerous IRA convicts were housed there.

Night news editor George Kerr needed to mobilise at least four reporters and two photographers for the fifty-mile trip to Portlaoise. Astonishingly, none of us could drive and therefore were unable to utilise the company's fleet of VW Beetles berthed in a car park in Hawkins Street. All George could do was hire a fleet of taxis to ferry us to the scene. With waiting time and return fares, the bill for covering the story for the cash-strapped *Press* was immense.

As a result, the management introduced a scheme of free driving lessons for reporters and photographers. For me, the timing couldn't have been better – the Dublin bus drivers had just begun what was to be a protracted strike.

Army lorries were introduced to bring commuters in from the suburbs, but the service was sketchy. I lived on Palmerston Road and found that waiting for an over-crowded military truck was just as time-consuming as a walk through Ranelagh, down Camden Street, past Trinity College to Burgh Quay.

But now, with free driving lessons, I could instruct the wallah from the Irish School of Motoring to pick me up at 7 a.m. from Palmerston Road, tutor me in three-point turns and gear changes and drop me at Burgh Quay in time for my 8 a.m. *Evening Press* shift.

In the afternoon, the process was reversed. After a refreshing pint or two in Mulligan's after my labours finished at 4 p.m., I was collected by the Irish School of Motoring for further tuition, concluding at my front door in Palmerston Road. This went on for the duration of the strike. I had at least thirty-five hours of driving lessons.

When I passed my driving test first time, I was held up by managing editor Bill Redmond as an example to all. That is, until the invoice arrived from the Irish School of Motoring. The bean counters in *Irish Press* accounts in Elephant House on O'Connell Street had failed to put a cap on the number of hours reporters could avail themselves of, and they were not happy with the cost of instructing young reporter McEntee.

From then on it was decreed that reporters and photographers seeking driving instruction would be entitled to a maximum of twelve lessons. Bill Redmond got revenge of a sort when another strike was subsequently called by the busmen later that year. I was put on a semi-permanent 9 a.m.–5 p.m. shift, a wasteland between the high activity of the *Evening Press* and too early for the courts and the Dáil. A sort of editorial Bermuda Triangle.

Redmond's scheme obliged me to walk or catch an

early army truck from Rathmines to the City Centre. I would then collect and drive one of the *Press*'s VW Beetles from the Hawkins Street garage to Redmond's semi-detached home in Sandymount.

Leaving the engine running, I would ring the front doorbell and wait for Mrs Redmond to hand me Bill's briefcase. I would then respectively hold both the gate and the front passenger seat of the VW open as the great man progressed from his front door down the garden path and into the car.

Bill was a very large man, rendered elephantine by the small confines of the Beetle. It was impossible to see any traffic on the passenger side. After the 25-minute drive, I would park at the back entrance to the *Press*, get out, open the passenger door, watch Redmond's jumbo rear climb the back stairway and return the car to the pool. When I reported for duty minutes later, Redmond would nod as though we hadn't met that day.

My chauffeur duties triggered much sniggering from Sharkey, Brendan Burke, Tom McPhail and Michael Keane, who had somehow wangled permanent positions on the *Evening Press* duty roster.

Ten years later, my driving let me down in Dublin. But then, I'll admit, drink had a lot to do with it. Stationed in London, I had returned home on holiday and motored up to Dublin in my yellow, high-powered, two-door Ford Cortina to meet Con Houlihan for a drink.

Con, 6 ft 6 in., was a brilliant sports writer among other talents and had an eccentricity of covering his face with his hand as he spoke. I met him and *Evening Press* editor Sean Ward in the Harp Bar near O'Connell Bridge.

I lingered the entire afternoon, drinking far too many pints of Smithwick on an empty stomach. Emerging in pouring rain at about 6 p.m. and facing a 72-mile drive back to Cavan, I weaved my way to Bewley's coffee and cake shop on Westmoreland Street and bought a splendid cake for my mother. I added half a dozen packs of King's excellent potato crisps to consume on the homeward journey.

Placing the cake and crisps on the front passenger seat, I pointed the car in the direction of Phoenix Park and motored down Eden Quay to follow the River Liffey to the Guinness Brewery and the gates of the park. The windscreen wipers could barely cope with the cascading rain and visibility was poor. That did not excuse, however, the sudden crunch of front bumper on back bumper as I collided with the car ahead, which had braked as the lights went red.

That car bumped the vehicle in front and that car collided with the back of the motor in front. All in all, three vehicles suffered damage from my Cortina. I got out, surveyed my broken headlight, damaged grill and number plate clinging to the Cortina by one screw. The back bumper of the car in front lay on the wet roadway and the boot lid was open. There was collateral but less severe damage to the other two cars.

The irate drivers surrounded me. I mumbled that all would be well and to send the repair bills to me. I found paper and pen and, inexplicably, wrote my name and address in Gaelic. Sean Mac an tSaoi, 61 Sraid ne H-Eglise, Cabhan, County Cabhan (Church Street, Cavan). The fact I actually lived in London was neither here nor there.

One of the drivers exclaimed, 'He's drunk! You can smell it off him.' Just then, a member of the Garda Síochána on foot patrol on O'Connell Street pushed through the gaggle of wet drivers to see what was holding up the traffic.

As the irate motorists explained what had happened, I made another mistake, saying too loudly to the policeman, 'I have a brother in the force', accompanied by a wink. This was the equivalent of lighting the blue touchpaper.

My younger brother Desmond was, in fact, a member of the Garda Síochána stationed in Monaghan.

Amid the uproar, I pointed a wet finger across the nearby River Liffey to the quayside offices of the *Irish*

Press, explaining I was the London correspondent of said newspaper and would pay for all the damage to the vehicles involved in the crash.

The Garda looked at me, then looked at the trio of drivers, then back to me. 'OK,' he said. 'If we go across to the *Irish Press* and someone can vouch for you and you agree to recompense these gentlemen, we'll see if that is OK with my sergeant in Store Street. I'll accompany you.'

As he hopped into the front passenger's seat of the car, there was a scrunching noise as he flattened the Bewley's cake and turned my King's potato crisps into sawdust.

Worse was to come. I turned left at O'Connell Bridge and left again at Burgh Quay. The Garda exclaimed, 'Jesus, John, I'm not sure if you are fit to drive. How much have you had to drink?' 'Two pints,' I lied.

As I pulled up at the pavement in front of the *Irish Press*, I could hear the clang and grind of the three damaged cars, bumpers askew, pulling in behind me. They were not letting me out of their sight.

I went into the neon-lit front office and mercifully spotted Sean, a former copy boy now manning the reception desk. I quickly explained my plight and asked him to come out and identify me in front of the Garda and the upset drivers. He did so to the satisfaction of the peeler.

The Garda then pointed back across the Liffey to Store Street Garda station. 'OK, now let's drive over there and I'll consult the sergeant.' I led the procession of bruised motors down Burgh Quay, turning left at Butt Bridge and halting outside Store Street. The Garda disappeared into the station. He was gone for about five minutes. He returned and leaned in the driver's window of my Cortina.

'The sergeant said that, on condition that you don't drive back to Cavan and satisfy these gentlemen that you will pay for the damage, you are free to go.'

Just then, there was a screech of brakes and a figure emerged from an old Renault and dramatically appeared at the Garda's shoulder. It was Tom Fallon, an *Irish Press* reporter and colleague who had just completed night classes to qualify as a barrister. He had been alerted by Sean at the front desk to my plight.

'It's all right, officer,' he barked. 'This man is my client. I represent him.' The policeman recoiled and said, 'Oh, that changes everything. I'll have to take him into custody.' I beckoned to Tom and whispered in his ear, 'Please fuck off, Tom, please.' He did.

I persuaded the guard to leave it at that and pledged universal repairs to the trio of disgruntled motorists. They handed over bits of paper containing their details and the policeman departed.

Waiting until the coast was clear, I then, shamefully, drove back to Cavan. A cascade of inflated garage bills followed as I financed the major refurbishment of three vehicles. Never again. (And I apologised to Tom.)

By 1973, I was a comparatively battle-hardened reporter. I had even survived offending the then coalition Minister for Post and Telegraphs Dr Conor Cruise O'Brien. His chum Mick O'Toole, deputy news editor on the *Evening Press*, had asked me to call him after a tip-off that he'd had all his teeth removed.

I called his Howth home. His wife, Maire Mac an tSaoi (no relation), answered the telephone. 'Could I speak to Dr O'Brien?' I asked. 'Who are you?' she replied. 'John McEntee from the *Evening Press*,' I said. 'What do you want?' she asked.

I explained: 'I understand the minister has had an operation on his teeth.' 'Hold on,' she countered and then, sotto voce, addressed her husband. 'Conor, you're wanted on the telephone.'

'Hello, who is this?' boomed the irritated Conor. 'It's John McEntee from the *Evening Press*.' 'What do you want?' 'I gather you have had all your teeth removed,' I said. 'What?'

'You've had all your teeth removed?' I repeated. 'No, no, I haven't. I have had a minor dental operation.' 'What sort of operation?' I enquired. 'A minor operation. How dare you? Can I speak to your superior?'

Now, in retrospect, I should have hung up, but I didn't. I summoned Mick O'Toole. 'Mick, the Cruiser would like a word.'

Mick grabbed the telephone and immediately stood to attention. 'Mick O'Toole, assistant news editor here. Dr O'Brien, can I help you? What? I quite understand, yes, of course. Good heavens. I can only apologise for his behaviour. Yes, I will, I am extremely sorry. Goodbye.'

I got the bollocking of all bollockings from Mick. But he had asked me to call the Cruiser.

By the time of Pope John Paul II's trip to Ireland in September 1979, I had been working as London correspondent for the *Irish Press* for four years. The visit was deemed sufficiently important to involve all the paper's reporting staff and I was brought back from exile to cover the pontiff's visit to the Marian shrine of Knock in County Mayo.

It was the first visit of a pontiff to Ireland (they'd had to make do with a Eucharistic Congress in 1932) and the entire country had gone pontiff crazy. My parents were mere specks at the papal Mass in the Phoenix Park attended by 1 million people (and a fortune was made nationwide by chancers selling folding canvas stools for the event).

Knock had, apparently, been visited by the Virgin Mary in the nineteenth century. It was Ireland's answer to Lourdes and Fátima and thousands had gathered for this once-in-a-lifetime event. The surrounding countryside was bedecked with tents and camper vans to accommodate the vast number of pilgrims who had slept overnight in anticipation of a sighting or meeting with Pope John Paul II.

I was assigned to cover the Mass for the sick in the impressive round basilica built by local priest Monsignor Horan (he was also responsible for the airport in the middle of nowhere).

At the last moment, the organisers decided that only the sick and their relatives could attend the Mass. No media would be admitted.

While the head of the Roman Catholic Church was delayed in nearby Galway by the soon-to-be-disgraced Bishop Eamon Casey at a joyful Mass for the youth of Ireland, I set about ensuring my presence at the Knock Mass.

In a bar outside the village I acquired a surplus wheelchair, a rug and a chauffeur for £20. Bargaining over where my newfound friend would berth me for the service cost me the price of four pints of Guinness. Needless to say, I had also consumed a similar amount while bartering. But more of that later.

He wheeled me to a spot at the foot of the steps to the altar. Before the Mass, the first shiver of self-doubt crept into my head as I surveyed my immediate neighbours. To my right was a child propped up on the pillow of a hospital bed, festooned with a drip and other life-supporting nourishments fed by tube. To my left was an extremely frail, porcelain-faced elderly lady slumped in sleep in her wheelchair. Other wheelchairs and beds were parked in a circle around the base of the raised altar. Behind me there were rows and rows of less ailing Mass goers.

The only attendees as healthy as me were the battalion of curates flitting about the basilica. Also not requiring any medical attention was the phalanx of formidable Handmaids of the Lord. (To call them Battleaxes of the Lord would not contravene the Trades Descriptions Act.)

This was a collection of burly, purple-faced women of a certain age, clearly recruited from local golf clubs and bridge schools. Sweet Afton cigarettes and Cork Dry Gin with Schweppes tonic seemed to be their weapons of choice. Their uniforms (think Matron Hattie Jacques in *Carry on Doctor*) were a mixture of the medical and religious, a blue shirt fronted by a large white apron, the breast of which displayed a large red-coloured crucifix.

As the Holy Father's helicopter could be heard mechanically clucking overhead, these women in unison moved through the basilica until they had taken up pole positions at the foot of the altar. As John Paul was landing outside, they had formed an impenetrable circle of nurse/nun invincibility that obscured the view of all the sick, including myself.

The priest in charge of Knock, Monsignor Horan, took to the stage – sorry, the altar – and declared, 'Will the Handmaids of the Lord move back, please, so that the sick can see His Holiness when he arrives?'

They refused to budge. Some even defiantly folded their arms. With a nod from Monsignor Horan, his black-soutaned Stormtroopers (the curates) moved forward in unison and began waving their hands at the women, shooing them back.

A few stepped back but eventually the curates had to resort to energetic pushing and shoving. Finally and grudgingly, the Handmaids surrendered the area around the altar and moved back two or three rows to allow the unwell (and me) to witness John Paul Ringo's arrival.

It was an impressive sight. The charismatic pontiff, dressed all in white, bounded up the steps to the altar and immediately clasped both hands triumphantly over his head. 'People of Ireland,' he boomed, 'I love you.'

He was two hours late but no one seemed to care (apart, perhaps, from the thousands outside who were denied the sight of John Paul in his planned Popemobile tour through the adjoining hills and fields – cancelled because of failing light).

As the Mass proceeded, the half-gallon of porter I had consumed while negotiating for my wheelchair began to take its toll. My bladder filled. I squirmed in the wheelchair. I became light-headed. Sweat appeared above my upper lip. I was in pain. If I hadn't been unwell before the pontiff arrived, I was now.

'Is there much more of this?' I wondered as His Holiness raised the Host. 'Body of Christ,' he declared. 'Christ' was all I answered.

Then, at last, the closing sign of peace. I tried to shake hands with my sleeping companion on one side and the comatose child in the bed on my other side. They were oblivious.

Then this rock star-like Pope was down among the beds and crutches and wheelchairs, clutching hands, embracing children, blessing anyone who caught his eye. I felt my hand being squeezed. It was Christ's Vicar on Earth, shaking my hand as he gazed down at me. 'God bless you, my son,' his deep voice boomed. Then he was gone. The heavens didn't open to reveal a celestial choir. But, as I wrote in the *Oldie* magazine, my bladder nearly did.

It was impossible not to be struck by the sheer power and vitality of the man. This was before he was almost fatally shot in St Peter's Square less than a year later. For a moment I forgot my urgent need to relieve myself.

But an earlier twinge had grown into full-blown guilt and shame. What on earth was I doing masquerading as an invalid amid the largest collection of genuinely sick people ever gathered in one spot in Irish history? All to be touched physically or emotionally by this very special Pope.

I waited until the basilica had emptied, waving away Handmaids and helpers who wished to wheel me out into the sunshine. A furtive glance left and right confirmed the coast was clear. I stood up, shed my rug and walked awkwardly out of the basilica in search of the nearest public convenience. Two years later, the Pope, now much reduced in vitality after being shot, arrived in London. I followed him from Westminster Cathedral to Canterbury on to Wembley Stadium, Manchester, Liverpool and Cardiff. The crowds were enormous during those summer Masses.

In Liverpool, I stood next to the protesting Ian Paisley and Peter Robinson as they shouted 'Anti-Christ, Satan of Rome'. They waved their Bibles at a street corner as the Popemobile carrying His Holiness proceeded from the Anglican Cathedral down the hill to Paddy's Wigwam, the Roman Catholic Cathedral.

As he passed the frothing Free Presbyterian clergymen, the Pope noticed Paisley and Robinson. He leaned forward and asked the driver to slow down. As he passed at a snail-like pace the 'Anti-Christ' serenely blessed Ian and Peter.

Also accompanying the Pope was a much more important and substantial figure, Paul Callan of the *Daily Mirror*. The portly, bow-tied Callan and I shared a booze-laden train from Euston to Liverpool Lime Street and had enjoyed a Bohemian night of further carousing at the once magnificent Adelphi Hotel, modelled on the interior of the doomed *Titanic*.

The next time I saw Callan was in Ambleside Avenue in Streatham, a former brothel occupied by Cynthia Payne, famously dubbed Madam Cyn. She had been jailed for providing sexual service for mature men, many of them members of the House of Lords, MPs and captains of industry.

To celebrate the publication of her ghosted memoir by Paul Bailey, I turned up at the former brothel for the party. Callan, surrounded by Madam Cyn's former call girls, bellowed, 'I haven't seen you since the Pope!'

On my arrival at her house, Cynthia Payne had answered the front door with a twinkle in her eye. Before

I had time to introduce myself, she slid her right-hand palm upwards between the legs of my Prince of Wales check suit trousers. Energetically patting upwards, she chuckled, 'Ooooh, you're a big boy, come in.'

I had come to interview her and subsequently stayed to enjoy a very raucous shindig with her working girls and curious customers.

In December 1978, police who raided Cynthia's suburban villa found fifty-three men huddled in the hall. Most were queuing on the stairs leading up to the bedrooms and were clutching luncheon vouchers to be redeemed for sex; some appeared to have come straight from the office. Of the thirteen women on the premises, some were completely naked. For £25, Cynthia offered mature clients (no one under forty was admitted) a lavish buffet, which included wine and sex with one of the girls she employed.

Most of her customers eschewed conventional sexual intercourse, preferring bondage, whipping, spanking – one delighted in being stripped, covered in honey and having one of Cynthia's ladies switch a vacuum from suck to blow, thus pebble dashing him with household dust.

Afterwards, the girls returned the vouchers to Cynthia and received £8 for each sexual chore. They invariably finished their shift with a snack of poached egg on toast and a hot cup of tea.

Cynthia, who died aged eighty-two in 2015, went to jail after the police raid (there were rumours the police action was triggered by Cynthia's failure to offer freebies to Streatham's PC Plods).

At her trial, she was ineradicably branded 'Madam Cyn' and imprisoned for eighteen months for running 'the biggest disorderly house' in British history.

'We had a high-class clientele,' Cynthia Payne recalled many years later. 'No rowdy kids, no yobs, all well-dressed men in suits who knew how to respect a lady. It was like a vicar's tea party with sex thrown in – a lot of elderly, lonely people drinking sherry.'

A rapt media feasted on stories of middle-aged and elderly men queuing up in SW16 for food, drink, conversation, striptease shows and a trip upstairs with the girl of their choice. Jeffrey Bernard in *The Spectator* declared her 'the greatest Englishwoman since Boadicea'.

On appeal, Cynthia's sentence was reduced to six months and a hefty fine. She was unrepentant, however, and on her release from prison she resumed her parties until the police called again in 1986.

When Cynthia, a jolly, roly-poly figure, let me into her home in 1982, it was furnished in a style of overwhelming suburban ordinariness, with nets at the windows, starched antimacassars and plenty of pretty china. We found a quiet room to conduct the interview. By the time we'd finished, the party was in full swing (I'd noticed the ice-laden bath upstairs was full of bottles of wine, vodka, brandy, Pernod and even sherry). The crowded front room was filled with Cynthia's former working girls. They all spoke with fondness of her. Many had been rescued from pimps and a grubby existence on street corners and loveless sexual commerce in the back of clients' motor cars.

Cynthia's imprisonment had forced many back to a life of exploitation. As a former prostitute herself, she understood and supported these working girls.

At the party, there was one elderly gent in a wheelchair who had been a regular attendee at the luncheon voucher parties (Cynthia made a point of gratifying invalids), a PVC-clad transvestite and a bewhiskered ex-RAF wing commander who told me, straight-faced, that he enjoyed trips to nearby Epping Forest, where one of Cynthia's scantily clad girls stripped him naked, blindfolded him and left him alone tied to a tree where he spent the afternoon excited by the prospect of discovery. Once, he joked, they'd forgotten about him until nightfall.

I stayed far too long and failed to notice the winking camera as I talked to a beautifully dressed transvestite and a bondage aficionado with stiletto-pointed breasts and a leather balaclava. I paid no attention to reporter John Stapleton recording a report for that night's edition of BBC2's *Newsnight*.

I arrived home just as *Newsnight* was starting on the TV in my suburban living room. 'Where have you been?' asked my long-suffering wife. As I mumbled gibberish about an important interview, she pointed excitedly at the TV. 'It's you! What are you doing?' I peered at the telly. Stapleton was delivering his pre-recorded piece on Madam Cyn's party. Behind him, in full view, glass in hand, head thrown back as I laughed at the tranny's joke, was yours truly. Needless to say, I did not mention Cynthia's opening remark.

Two years later, I found myself yet again temporarily out of work due to industrial action by the NUJ in the Dublin office.

I sought shift work at *The Sun* in Bouverie Street. I was struck by the dapper elegance of staff members like John Kay, who arrived each morning wearing well-cut suits, clutching umbrellas and briefcases like City gents (I subsequently discovered that their opposite numbers at *The Guardian* wore casual trousers, open-neck shirts and trainers).

The day after comedian Tommy Cooper crumpled and died suddenly and publicly on the stage of Her

Majesty's Theatre in the West End in April 1984, just before the commercial break of an ITV variety show, I found myself standing on the pavement outside his home in Barrowgate Road in Chiswick. I had been dispatched by *Sun* news editor Tom Petrie to secure an interview with Mrs Cooper.

I watched as rival reporters were rebuffed by the Filipino maid at the doorstep of the six-bedroom, mock-Tudor, semi-detached house. I decided to take a wander up Chiswick High Street, have a beer and return later. When I did, laden with flowers and full of the bonhomie induced by four foaming pints of London Pride ale, the coast was clear.

I rang the doorbell and took a deep breath.

The maid appeared, repeating mantra-like that Mrs Cooper was not seeing anyone. As she spoke I could see across her left shoulder the top of the grey hair of Mrs Cooper's head, her red-rimmed eyes blinking behind enormous spectacles. 'What lovely flowers!' she exclaimed, elbowing her way alongside the maid. I asked if she would accept the flowers as a token of sympathy from readers of *The Sun*.

'Are you Irish?' she asked. I answered in the affirmative and was immediately invited into the open-plan front hall.

Poignantly, at the foot of the stairs was a large wooden trunk bound with leather straps. It contained Tommy's props from the night before. It had been delivered earlier by a factotum from London Weekend Television. He hadn't stayed to field the telephone calls of sympathy to a bewildered Mrs Cooper or prevent an opportunistic Irish journalist from gaining entry to the house of mourning.

Atop the trunk was what appeared to be a half-consumed sliced pan loaf. Mrs Cooper – 'call me Dove' – pointed at it and explained, 'It's Tommy's banana sandwiches. He always took a whole loaf of banana sandwiches when he was on stage.' She dissolved in floods of tears, adding, 'He's only eaten half of them.'

It was at about this time I realised that Tommy's widow was more than well lubricated. Dove beckoned to a collection of bottles on a table near the TV. She asked me to pour her a large Gordon's gin with Schweppes tonic water.

'Have one yourself, love,' she added. I did. As I busied myself with the cocktails, the telephone rang in the open-plan dining room. 'Would you answer that, love?' she asked. I lifted the receiver. It was fellow comic Eric Morecambe, calling to pay his respects. Mrs Cooper shook her head in the negative to indicate she didn't want to take the call. 'I'm sorry, Mrs Cooper is indisposed,' I said in a gravelly voice.

Over the next few hours I fielded calls from Michael Parkinson, Eric Sykes, Ronnie Barker, Barry Cryer and a profusion of the late Tommy's other acquaintances.

His widow then asked if I would sit with her and watch the video of his last show from the previous evening. After refreshing our drinks, we sat on a sofa together and turned on the TV and video. Dove wept profusely throughout, while periodically nudging me with her empty glass, which I refilled repeatedly. When Tommy came on the TV screen, she virtually howled and, babbling incoherently, pointed at the uneaten sandwiches atop his trunk in the nearby hall. 'He never even finished his banana sandwiches!' she wailed.

When Tommy, wearing an Egyptian full-length smock, collapsed on stage (the audience obviously thought it was part of his act), she asked me to freeze the frame. At her insistence, we watched it again and again. She became even more upset.

Finally she'd had enough and we switched off the TV. I was mercifully distracted by the telephone. Then she asked if I could take the trunk to the first floor. I removed the sandwiches and half pushed and hauled the trunk up the stairs. All of the bedrooms apart from Tommy and Dove's master bedroom were full to the rafters with props for Tommy's magic tricks. There was the famous full-sized guillotine (which, inebriated, he demonstrated on the *Parkinson* show, almost decapitating the chat-show host), plastic ducks, bows and arrows, guns and furry toys. I found a space in a spare bedroom and pushed the trunk in behind the door.

Later all this paraphernalia would be sold at auction. Ade Edmondson paid a staggering £7,000 for what transpired to be mostly junk, bits of glass and plastic diminished by the absence of the bumbling genius magician who had lovingly assembled the collection of novelties and tricks. Craig Brown recently disclosed that he had paid £110 for a number of suitcases containing Tommy's plastic flowers, admitting that they have given him much pleasure.

But all this was in the future. As was the disclosure that Tommy had a long-time mistress in his personal assistant Mary Kay and that, in his drink-befuddled state, he would occasionally beat Dove up. On this day it was clear she adored him and was devastated by his death.

She insisted on showing me the self-contained flat they had built at the back of the house for their son Tommy Jr – now dead as well.

I opened an overhead wall unit in the kitchen and an avalanche of Tommy's trademark fezzes of various sizes cascaded out and dropped onto the floor. It was surreal.

This fez tsunami triggered more grief-stricken caterwauling from Dove. I had now been with Mrs Cooper for more than three hours.

Then Tommy's daughter, an alarming doppelgänger of her dad, arrived and eyed me suspiciously. 'What are you doing here?' she asked. I had no answer.

Dove and I were sitting at the scarred and pock-marked mahogany dining-room table where Tommy painstakingly practised all his magic tricks (including the famous ever-expanding Martini bottle). 'He got the tricks to perfection and then deliberately messed them up,' explained Dove. I knew it was time to go. When I returned to *The Sun*'s newsroom in Bouverie Street, Tom Petrie asked me how I'd got on. 'She wouldn't talk to me,' I lied. I just hadn't the heart to write it all up for the delectation of *Sun* readers.

Another *Sun* shift included my being dispatched with a photographer to London's East End, where an attractive mother of two had sent her photo to *The Sun* after winning the Miss Darndale beauty contest in a local shopping centre.

A wholesome, well-upholstered brunette, she admitted the pair of us while her twelve-year-old son and his chum sat in a back room watching a video of the film *Flash Gordon*.

The photographer immediately tut-tutted at the modest, buttoned-up blouse she was wearing under her kitchen apron. After I had scribbled down the necessary details for a caption, he somehow persuaded her to allow him to accompany her upstairs to choose a more appropriate outfit from her wardrobe for the *Sun* photograph. I remember thinking it was a form of hypnosis. She seemed to have lost her free will.

I joined the boys watching Brian Blessed in *Flash Gordon* until the photographer summoned me with a yell to the front room to help with his picture. He asked me to stand against the wall holding aloft one of his flash guns. I was astonished at the transformation of this sweet, suburban housewife and mother.

Sitting on the arm of the sofa, she had her tight black skirt hitched up to suspender-belt level. Displaying acres of leg encased in black fishnet stockings, she leaned forward with the fingers of her right hand cupped around her chin.

A white, elasticised top clung on for dear life just above her nipples, showing a Grand Canyon of cleavage. Her hair, previously in a bun, now cascaded down to her shoulders. 'Lovely, lovely,' purred the photographer as he snapped away. As I stood rigid against the wall, my right hand held aloft holding the flash, I had a disturbing vision of her husband coming home unexpectedly and landing both myself and the snapper in the A&E department of the nearest hospital.

Driving back to Fleet Street, the photographer boasted, 'Another ten minutes and I would have had her topless.' The following day, my completely rewritten story accompanied a lurid shot of Miss Darndale under the headline, 'Come on, folks. Have you a mum as sexy as this?'

Normal service soon resumed with resolution of the industrial action in Dublin. By then I had been nine years in London. Between strikes it was a dream job. Apart from reporting events from London for the trio of papers in Burgh Quay, I could exploit my interest in literature, films and art by interviewing big names who visited the British capital – no one then bothered including Dublin in the itinerary for a famous novelist or film star.

I had lunch with Norman Mailer, tea with Iris Murdoch, numerous drinks with Anthony Burgess, chats with Paul Newman, Jimmy Stewart, Bette Davis, Muhammad Ali, Meryl Streep, Mick Jagger, John Travolta, Sean Connery, Joan Collins, Lee Marvin, Gore Vidal, Sidney Sheldon and James Mason.

To be candid, I was too young and immature to fully appreciate these one-to-one encounters with what were then the most famous and gifted people on the planet.

Not included in that litany of greatness is Doris Stokes, a medium who was coining it by claiming that she could contact the dead. He books, commencing with *Voices in My Ear*, had been bestsellers. Doris specialised in contacting dead children, reassuring distraught parents that their departed offspring were happy and waiting for them on the other side.

She thrived in the post-Christian era, where the doctrines preached by clergymen, mullahs and rabbis were not only found to be flawed, but no one believed them any more.

Doris Stokes was a medium people believed in. Thousands flocked to the dumpy, middle-aged housewifely figure from Grantham who guaranteed reassuring contact with dead loved ones. Few left disappointed after matronly Doris made a ship-to-shore call to paradise and poured soothing balm on grief.

She's been dead for about a quarter of a century but is still remembered by devotees. Eamonn Holmes believed in her and Harry Enfield developed a Doris Stokes character for one of his TV shows.

Of course, she was a charlatan, but a well-meaning one. I don't believe she did any harm pretending to convey messages from the grave. She gave more comfort to grieving parents, daughters and sons than a Vatican full of rosary-bead-waving monsignors ever could. She filled both the London Palladium and Sydney Opera House and was the most famous spiritualist in the last quarter of the twentieth century.

I met her in her council flat off the Fulham Road where she lived with her husband John. She was promoting a follow-up to *Voices in My Ear*.

The sitting room was dominated by chunky armchairs and a large sofa poised before a widescreen TV. Unmissable on an otherwise bare wall was a square of cheap wood surmounted by a triangle and capped with a wooden crucifix.

Inside the square was a noticeboard-style jumble of more than 100 snapshots; some curling upwards, others pinned down, many yellowing at the edges.

All of them were of children. Pre-teens in Boy Scout and Girl Guide outfits. Others caught in the glare of sunshine on family holidays in Clacton, Eastbourne, Spain, France, Florida and other venues. All smiling, all happy – all dead. 'Who are they?' I asked Doris. 'Oh, these are my spirit children. I am in touch with them all.'

Distraught parents, despairing of conventional religion, contacted Doris to ask if she could get in touch with their offspring tragically and brutally taken from them before they could really start a life. Doris asked them to forward photographs. As far as I know, no money changed hands. Doris made contact and reported back to broken fathers and mothers that their Dominics and Lauras, Tristrams and Zoes were fine and happy on the other side.

How could I mock? Traditional clergy had consoled them with nonsense about God's Will and some mysterious grand plan. How could the drowning of an eight-year-old or the loss of a five-year-old to cancer be God's will?

Doris, I have no doubt, helped these people with their grief. But there I must draw a line. Doris spouted an extraordinary theory. In the afterlife, she claimed, children grew to adulthood and frail OAPs became younger. She had lost a son – his sepia-tinted image adorned her TV – surely he was still a little boy in paradise?

'No, no,' she insisted. 'He will have grown up.' To her consternation, I carried her theory to its logical conclusion. If her elderly parents were growing younger and her baby son was growing up, surely at some stage they would be the same age.

This confused and annoyed her. I changed the subject. We had a similar stand-off when I suggested that she might have some pre-knowledge of the people who flocked to her sell-out rallies. It had been claimed that when grief-stricken relatives contacted her or her husband John they were invited to elaborate on the person who had died. Names, interests, hobbies and passions. They were then given free tickets to the next clairvoyant shindig where she would astonish the rest of the audience with her inside knowledge.

'I am getting a message from Albert,' she would intone from the stage, eyes closed and hands reaching out into the auditorium. 'He recently passed away. He is anxious that his allotment is looked after and his wife – yes, I can hear a name, his wife Margaret – he says she must not be too sad.'

From the well of the audience a hand would rise in excitement and gratitude. 'I'm Margaret. I lost Albert in February.' The auditorium would indulge in a collective intake of breath admiring the skill of Doris. Little did they know that Mr and Mrs Stokes were already au fait with the plight of Margaret.

In other circumstances, Mrs Stokes would vaguely mention a name: 'I am getting a message from George, no, Georgina, no, it's Gilbert...' Eventually there would be a shriek and a hand would be raised. 'It must be my George!'

Inevitably George would come through to say he didn't like the colour of the new wallpaper in the bedroom (how many people redecorate the bedroom after a bereavement?) or he was annoyed about the old suit-case on the top of the wardrobe in the spare room (ditto). I noted that the spirits who monopolised the ear of Doris Stokes never imparted the name or number of the Grand National winner or the six digits that would win the roll-over in Wednesday's National Lottery.

The information was of no consequence. Personally, I feel if I had the ability to contact the living from heaven or wherever, I would impart information that might prove useful. Don't visit Christchurch, New Zealand, in February – there will be an earthquake. Do not shop in the market district of Baghdad during your forth-coming holiday. That sort of thing.

The final irony was her own demise. She knew she was ill and left precise instructions to her manager Laurie O'Leary. Her book royalties were large. She told him that she would make contact from the other side and give her instructions.

She never did. She died in 1987 and there hasn't been a supernatural squeak from her since.

Her manager, bereft of precise guidance, continued to cash in from her name and back catalogue. Who could blame him? He told me that the moment Doris imparted her instructions, he would carry them out. He died six years ago without receiving a single message from his client. I'd like to think that on his arrival on the other side, Doris had more than a word in his ear.

* * *

Drink was an important part of life at the *Irish Press* London redoubt, where we boasted three wiremen to tip-tap our copy via ticker tape machine to Dublin. Permanently thirsty, they were usually in the Old Bell when the towels came off the beer taps at 11 a.m. Clive the apprentice didn't last long and Jack Craddock finally got his wish to return to the mother ship in Burgh Quay before the *Irish Press* group folded in 1995.

But London lad John Stephenson was at the *Irish Press* man and boy, even surviving the closure of the wire room. He was like the son bachelor London editor Aidan Hennigan never had.

With little to do after the wire room closure, he was put in charge of the fax machine. I would write my copy on the office typewriter, handing the copy to John, who would send it to Dublin via fax. Journalists were not permitted to fax directly except in an emergency or at weekends.

John had a talent for brewing his own superior hooch at home in Walthamstow. Frequently he arrived in the office at 8 a.m. with his own brand of Southern Comfort, crème de menthe or Drambuie. The litre of contraband would be polished off before pub opening.

London editor Aidan did not participate in the daily alcoholic carnival. His weakness was jam or, if he felt particularly decadent, honey. Consequently, the desks, chairs, door handles and the wall-mounted telephones were permanently sticky as a result of Aidan's addiction. One year, he promised to forsake his jam habit for the forty days of Lent. His girlfriend Kate telephoned one day and asked if here was any evidence of jam or honey consumption in the office. 'Of course not,' I insisted as my hand was superglued to the telephone receiver with remnants of Robertson's finest strawberry preserve.

When the *Press* switched from the outdated wire machine to fax in the mid '80s, senior NGA man Paddy O'Brien was dispatched from the Dublin wire operation to supervise the transition. The idea was to somehow retain the old-fashioned open telephone line utilised by the wire, avoiding BT charges for the fax.

The job should have taken a few days. Paddy was with us for over two weeks. The reason? John Stephenson's homemade booze offerings. 'Fancy some Southern Comfort?' John would ask the immaculately besuited and waistcoated figure of Paddy first thing in the morning.

A week later, returning from an assignation at the nearby Old Bailey, I discovered the prone figure of Paddy spread across the stained carpet tiles, screwdriver in hand, resting on the cable atop the skirting.

His trademark brown Trilby hat was still on his head. 'How's it goin', Paddy?' I asked. Silence. I asked again. Silence. Had he suffered a heart attack?

I walked across the room and kneeled beside him. He was unconscious – snoring. Just then, John popped his head around the door to the adjoining room clutching a litre-sized lemonade bottle and declared brightly: 'Oh, I think Paddy has had a little bit too much of my crème de menthe. Fancy some?'

On the day of his departure, we brought Paddy across to the *Daily Telegraph* pub, the King & Keys, for a farewell drink.

Standing at the bar, Paddy expressed his pleasure at returning to Dublin: 'You know,' he confided, 'I've enjoyed me time here. Great. But I miss the wife. Do you know something? We've been married forty-one years and in all that time I've never known her to vomit. Oh, she gags a bit after a few jars, but vomit? No. Never.'

Paddy was wearing the look dog-lovers assume when proudly boasting of Rover's ability to sit up and beg.

When Paddy was explaining his wife's remarkable

ability to desist from vomiting, Andy, the King & Keys barman was in the midst of topping up a pint of Courage Best bitter. He froze mid-pull. He looked at Paddy. Then he looked at John and I. He silently shook his head. Then he looked down and concentrated fiercely on finishing the foaming pint.

The King & Keys was our local also, shared by *Daily Telegraph* staff, led by editor Bill Deedes and blind leader writer T. E. Utley, next door.

The manager was an amiable Limerick man, Mark O'Donnell. When he was transferred to an ale house near Oxford Circus, Aidan decreed that we have a whip-round and purchase a silver-plated tankard to present to Mark on his departure from Fleet Street.

At a very liquid event in Mark's new pub, Aidan delivered a charming speech before handing over the tankard to Mark. Hardly had Mark finished thanking the assembly than Aidan whipped the drinking vessel out of his hands, declaring, 'We have to get it engraved.'

The next day, my late colleague David Brazil was dispatched to an engravers near Ludgate Circus with the tankard and a handwritten note from Aidan, which declared, 'To Mark O'Donnell on the Occasion Of His Departure from the King & Keys from all his friends in Fleet Street.'

A crestfallen Brazil returned to Aidan and said, 'The engraver says the cost of the message will be twice the price of the tankard.'

Aidan made an executive decision to postpone the engraving. He dumped the tankard in an empty filing cabinet next to the wire room where all our copy was ticker-taped to Burgh Quay by Jack Craddock and John Stephenson.

The forlorn mug lay forgotten for some time until David Brazil was dispatched to head office at Burgh Quay for three months and was replaced by top reporter Des Nix.

At David's farewell do, described in Fleet Street lingo as a holiday ale, I resurrected the mug and symbolically presented it to Brazil. After the photograph, I dumped it back in the filing cabinet. Poor Aidan did not find the stunt the least bit amusing. Infrequently colleagues reported sightings of Mark in his new pub wondering what had happened to his commemorative mug. In fact, six months after he left the King & Keys, I encountered him and his delightful wife at an Irish shindig at the Tara Hotel in Kensington. Sheepishly he enquired after the tankard. 'Still at the engravers,' I lied. 'I'll chase it up.'

More time passed and the day came when Des Nix was obliged to resume his duties at head office. Another holiday ale was arranged. I retrieved the tankard from the filing cabinet. Accompanied by a short speech, I presented the silver-plated treasure to Des. Immediately after the photograph, I grabbed the tankard and popped it back into the filing cabinet.

By now beer had probably doubled in price since that happy evening when Mark O'Donnell was first presented and then deprived of his memorial.

Peter Marriott had joined the staff of the London office and, in time-honoured fashion, was given sight of the mug in a ceremony before his departure to Dublin for familiarisation and indoctrination. By now the tankard was tarnished and dented.

It was even briefly presented to Con Houlihan after his foreign assignment at the Cheltenham Gold Cup. I retrieved it from his big Kerry paws before he headed to the Kings & Keys for his traditional brandy flavoured with milk.

But London editor Aidan did not welcome enquiries about the long-delayed engraving. If truth be told, he was embarrassed by the light-hearted guest appearances of the ageing ornament.

Its last sighting was on the return to Dublin of Isobel Conway, who, like her predecessors, had distinguished herself in the service of the *Irish Press* in the British capital. After the ale, a speech and ritual photograph, the silver-plated tankard disappeared for the last time into the filing cabinet.

On her departure from the staff of the *Irish Times* in the early '80s to live off her royalties, Maeve Binchy enquired about the tankard. 'I'd love to be presented with it,' she told me.

By then it had become the Fleet Street equivalent of the Holy Grail – this dinged, tarnished silver-plated tankard, drenched in the history of Irish journalism in the Street of Shame three decades ago.

I recently discovered that Aidan, now lost in the fug of Alzheimer's, did have the tankard inscribed and gave it to Mark before his death a few years ago.

Mark's successor at the King & Keys was his eccentric deputy Andy. Morose and shy, he was not suited for the hospitality industry. When the Australian cricket team visited the pub to promote a new lager, Castlemaine XXXX, I suggested writing a piece for the *Irish Press* along the lines of 'London Irish publican welcomes Aussie Cricket Heroes'. Andy declined, saying, 'My mother doesn't know I'm in England.' He then pondered for a while, after which he agreed, saying, 'OK, you can write something. If she gets in touch I'll say it is a case of mistaken identity.'

Among Andy's regulars were a gaggle of middle-aged, under-employed men who worked as messengers at the nearby *Daily Telegraph*. They spent most of their daylight hours propping up the long, narrow bar.

On one occasion, a pigeon limped into the King & Keys and was lifted to the counter by one of the *DT* messengers. Andy took a keen interest. The messenger diagnosed a broken wing. Andy opened the till, thrust a £20 note in the messenger's hand and told him to take a taxi to the Blue Cross animal hospital in Victoria, where the bird could be mended. Three of the messengers departed with the stricken bird. Instead of hailing a taxi, they went across Fleet Street to the Punch Tavern where they proceeded to drink Andy's taxi money.

Well-refreshed, they returned mid-afternoon with the bird and told Andy that the pigeon merely required rest. Andy tenderly took the bird from the messengers and brought it upstairs to the small flat above the bar, where he lay it down on his sofa bed and returned to his pint-pulling duties.

As Andy barely spoke to any of the *Irish Press* corps, I enquired of one of the messengers a few days later how the pigeon was progressing. He beckoned me out onto the street where he explained, 'The pigeon is dead.' I asked what had occurred. 'Andy had a few too many and after closing time he went upstairs in the dark and threw himself onto the sofa bed. He crushed the poor bird to death.'

While our little first-floor office was an engine room of news and feature-gathering for the three Dublin titles, *Sunday*, *Evening* and *Irish Press*, it could have been on the moon so detached was it from the rest of Fleet Street.

One afternoon I journeyed to Sloane Square to interview playwright Ron Hutchinson, whose *Rat in the Skull* was about to open at the Royal Court.

Over a drink in the bar next door, we got to talking about the modus operandi of the London office of the *Irish Press*. I explained the need to parochialise every British story, to find an Irish angle (it wasn't hard at the time with the IRA bombing British cities and the Central Criminal Court awash with Guildford and Birmingham bomb suspects). For example, I told him, a recent strike at the Willesden bus depot affected the huge Irish population living in Willesden, Harlesden and Kilburn. My story in the *Dublin Evening Press* was on the front page under the headline 'Thousands of Irish Walk to Work'.

Ron was so intrigued he went off and penned a BBC radio play about our antics. I found it difficult to explain to my boss Aidan why BBC boffins arrived to measure his office (he was played by the late T. P. McKenna).

Subsequently in London I was affected more by car

bombs and the brutal and indiscriminate use of the Prevention of Terrorism Act, which reduced the Irish population to mute fear. It was a velvet-voiced Irish nun called Sister Sarah who caused me most anxiety over the Act. Each time she telephoned, I feared imminent arrest. I knew the telephones at the *Irish Press* London office on Fleet Street were tapped. Sarah, a middle-aged, bespectacled creature who resided with her French order at a posh school in Kentish Town, had a hotline to the IRA.

When one bomber, Gerard Twohig, escaped from Brixton and featured on wanted posters up and down Britain, Sister Sarah rang. 'Great news, Mr McEntee. Gerry's safely home. I spoke to him today; he is mending cars at his father's garage in Mountnugent.'

And, after the ending of the Balcombe Street siege in 1975, when a gang of four IRA fanatics were cornered in a flat near Marylebone Station, Sister Sarah summoned me to her convent.

With the sound of schoolgirls singing hymns in the nearby chapel, she sat at a polished mahogany table and explained in detail how the Balcombe Street Four were about to confess to the Guildford and Woolwich pub bombings of 1974.

This was sensational stuff. Three men and a woman had been jailed for life for these atrocities. In addition, nearly the entire family of Annie Maguire, herself included, had been given long jail sentences for making the bombs that ripped through the pubs in Guilford and Woolwich.

'They didn't do it,' lisped Sister Sarah in that soothing nun's voice. 'It was the Balcombe Street boys that did. The Brits, Mr McEntee, are bastards.' She was right about the miscarriage of justice.

Shortly after I arrived in London to work for the *Irish Press*, a Coventry IRA prisoner Frank Stagg went on hunger strike in Wakefield Prison and subsequently died. My colleague David Brazil, who had very nationalistic views, befriended Frank's sister, a nurse in Coventry, during his final fast – so much so that he was sleeping with her. When he died, Brazil was shacked up with Ms Stagg and to contact him I had to call, let the phone ring three times and then call again. It was ludicrous – a journalist with the *Irish Press* protecting the sister of a newsworthy IRA martyr.

The plane carrying Frank's body home for burial was diverted by the government from Dublin, where a large IRA march was planned, to Shannon, where there would be less fuss.

The family and supporters were on another aeroplane, which landed in Dublin as scheduled. One of the relatives was Stagg's sister, accompanied by Brazil, who fended off Irish journalists keen to speak to her. My late colleague Seán MacConnell, based in the Dublin newsroom, recognised Brazil on the TV news and called me: 'You'd better have a word with Brazil. We can't have an *Irish Press* journalist shielding Stagg's sister from the press. It isn't right.'

When the SAS shot dead two IRA men and a woman in Gibraltar in 1987, thwarting the planting of a car bomb but prompting justifiable allegations of shooting three unarmed civilians, I was dispatched to the tiny British outpost to cover the aftermath.

Fleet Street's finest were holed up in the island's Holiday Inn, led by the great Ted Oliver from the *Daily Mail*. I was considered odd for wanting to leave the comfort of the hotel bar and ask some questions about the killings the day before. I found the local undertaker who had dealt with the bodies and contradicted the SAS contention that the trio had been felled with one bullet each to the head. 'How you say?' the Spanish Gibraltarian said. 'They were riddled!'

Back at the hotel, Ted had invented a fourth IRA suspect who had escaped. Donna Maguire was her name. At the time she was believed to be in Germany and was wanted for suspect bombings and killings. There was absolutely no evidence that Donna had been involved in the bid to bomb Gibraltar. 'It doesn't matter,' explained Ted. 'She's on the run. We have her photograph. She's good looking and she won't sue.'

The following morning, Ted's fiction appeared on the front page of the *Mail*. It also made the front pages of *The Sun*, *Express* and *Star*. And when this nonsense was picked up by the Press Association, it ran on the front page of the *Irish Press* in Dublin, only after I'd been bollocked for missing the story.

It was not comfortable being Irish in London in the late '70s and through the '80s. IRA atrocities committed in my name and in the name of all Irish people caused anti-Irish feeling at all levels. The Prevention of Terrorism Act struck its own terror into the entire Irish community, who feared arrest and detention on a whim.

But it was the bombings and killings in Birmingham, London, Manchester and other centres that caused the emigrant community much grief. And when the IRA murdered Lord Mountbatten in County Sligo in 1979, there was a particular outpouring of abuse aimed at the Irish. It was mostly subtle rather than overt. Take Kathleen, a lady from County Kerry, who disinfected the telephones in our Fleet Street office once a week (no one does that any more).

She could talk for Munster. For twenty years she'd

been wearing a pink coat disinfecting the office telephones in a stretch from the west side of St Paul's Cathedral, down Ludgate Hill and into Fleet Street.

On one particular day she reached my small bureau opposite the *Daily Telegraph* and was remarkably silent. No enquiries about the Kerry football team's Sunday triumph, no complaints about the cost of living back home. It was the morning after the IRA had murdered Lord Mountbatten in his lobster boat off the Sligo coast.

Eventually, as she tidied away her aerosol spray and unguent and shammy, she said, 'I've been in offices today where I've known people for over twenty years. I ask about their children and grandchildren. They enquire about mine. Today, wherever I went there was silence. No one would speak to me. Some deliberately turned their back on me.' Visibly distressed, Kathleen began to weep.

Throughout the course of the Troubles, there was one extraordinary Irishman, Sir Terry Wogan, broadcasting to an audience of 8 million on BBC Radio 2. Terry, who sadly died of cancer in January 2016, showed our British hosts that most Irish were decent, peace-loving neighbours who abhorred the actions of the IRA as much as they did.

Many Britons saw myself and other white-collar Irish residents as fifth columnists. Maybe we didn't plant bombs or kill people, but we silently supported the IRA. This was not the case but I recall Scotland Yard officers, barristers and even colleagues on English titles being less than helpful as I went about the course of my normal work.

One politician who was always tremendously helpful was the late Anthony Wedgwood Benn. Few of his obituaries in 2014 mentioned his sense of humour, but I think for a lot of his earnest socialist time on earth he was laughing inside. He thought it hilarious that *The Sun*, in advance of the 1982 election, summoned a clairvoyant who contacted the dead Stalin (not in heaven, surely) who roundly endorsed Wedgie as his kind of politician. How Tony laughed!

I recall visiting him in the early '80s at his handsome villa in Holland Park to talk about a book he'd written advocating a united Ireland. There was no one else in the tumbledown house with its faded rugs, battered furniture and antiquated kitchen. He had his trademark pipe and steaming mug of tea. Would I like a cup of tea? 'Yes,' I replied. He beckoned me to follow him into the kitchen where he put the kettle on and proceeded to instigate an elaborate search for a cup. A glass-fronted dresser stretched to the ceiling containing a collection of pink, willow-patterned crockery including at least four cups.

None possessed a handle. Eventually Wedgie located a large, badly chipped willow-pattern vessel. 'Would you mind having your tea in a sugar bowl?' he asked as he spooned loose tealeaves into a teapot. I didn't. When he had filled the sugar bowl to the brim with tea, he nodded and I followed his directions to a sofa in the front room where I sat, notebook in hand, facing him, my tea cooling on the coffee table. Every time I fancied a sip, I had to put down my pen and paper, reach over and lift the bowl and negotiate it to my lips, avoiding the series of lethal chips. I had to hold it like a chalice and each time Wedgwood Benn would immediately disappear from my view. On every occasion I returned the bowl to the table I could see a barely repressed chuckle behind Wedgie's po-face. He was, you might say, having a laugh.

(PS: Not quite so mirthful that he didn't tape our interview; his winking machine was sitting alongside my chipped sugar bowl on the table.)

Apart from covering momentous events such as the IRA bombing campaign, the Yorkshire Ripper trial, the election of Margaret Thatcher and the wedding of Charles and Diana, I had the privilege of interviewing a distinguished gallery of writers who would not have had Dublin on their book publicity tours.

Among them was *Roots* author Alex Haley. He was

particularly stressed when I met him at the Dorchester Hotel. The *Sunday Times* had just exposed his research into Kunta Kinte, the African slave whose journey he chronicled in the bestselling book. He was running about the suite like a headless chicken, fielding calls from US papers and TV channels seeking an explanation. Pursued by an assistant clutching a telephone, he suddenly halted and declared, 'You know that I am just as Irish as I am African?'

He explained that the granddaughter of Kunta Kinte, the original slave, had been raped on a Southern plantation by the owner. He had been born in County Monaghan. The resulting baby, Alex's great-grandfather, was half Irish!

He had found confirmation of his Irish ancestry in the parish records of a small Protestant church in Monaghan. As he was in the area for the weekend, the local vicar asked if he would meet the congregation at service on Sunday.

Alex recalled, 'He asked me to stay in the vestry and addressed the faithful. "I'd like you to meet a Protestant from America." I walked out. They were astonished. Most of them had never seen a black man.'

PART 3

FREELANCE

Before being dispatched to London in 1975, I had become inured to the all-too-frequent wildcat strikes in the militant Dublin newsroom. They continued while I represented the *Irish Press* in London, meaning that we downed typewriters in our London outpost. For some reason, strike pay and social welfare supplements were more generous in Ireland. Once, with a ravenous mortgage and two young children – another one would arrive afterwards – I presented myself at the Neasden dole office.

Accompanied by my colleague Aidan Hennigan, who treated the queue of tattooed supplicants, Rastas with ghetto blasters and shaven-headed yobs as some sort of social gathering, we explained our plight. Two weeks later, I received a cheque for £15. I still have it somewhere.

The means of survival during these disputes was to find casual shift work in the Fleet Street village. During one month-long strike, a former colleague from the *Irish Press* Diane Chanteau introduced me to Nigel Reynolds, who worked on the *Evening Standard*'s Londoner's Diary. Decently, he got me regular shifts on the feature. Geoffrey Wheatcroft was the patrician Diary editor, striking terror for some reason into the heart of the Oscar Wilde-like fellow casual John Walsh.

Perpetually listening to opera on his headphones as he rattled out a review for another publication, Geoffrey was not cut out for either gossip or editing. Approaching him with a tit-bit usually triggered a cessation of typing, a lifting of one of the headphones away from the ear and the injunction, 'John, is it terribly, terribly important?

Nothing ever was. Geoffrey didn't last as a gossip columnist. When he subsequently married the daughter of TV satirist Frank Muir, my *Standard* colleague Peter McKay quipped, 'Geoffrey has wed the *Call My Bluff* heiress.'

When industrial action in Dublin ceased, I would return to work at the *Irish Press*, supplementing my small income by selling stories to the *Standard* and to the late Peter Tory's quixotic and bizarrely located diary in the tabloid *Daily Star*.

My appearance against Richard Harris on behalf of the *Daily Star* (of which more later) did not enhance my career prospects with the *Irish Press*. I had worked with the paper in Dublin and London for a total of sixteen years and was disappointed to discover my departure would merit a redundancy figure of only £16,000.

But Richard Addis, who had succeeded Wheatcroft on the Diary, had promised me a job. However, just before I jumped ship, he was replaced by the affable Mark Jones. He agreed to honour the job pledge so I handed in my notice to Mr de Valera and reported for work at the new HQ of the *Standard*, Northcliffe House, above Barkers department store in Kensington. Naively, I had not felt any anxiety at the absence of a contract or written confirmation of my new role as a gossip columnist. Alarmingly, Mark Jones was clearing his desk the morning I arrived in January 1988. 'I've been fired,' he explained, pointing down the newsroom towards the office of editor John Leese. 'What about me?' I selfishly bleated. Mark simply shrugged.

Peter McKay, already a Fleet Street legend and former editor of the famed William Hickey column on the *Daily*

Express, had been parachuted in to temporarily run the troubled Diary. I explained my circumstances. Peter nodded sympathetically, told me, frankly, he couldn't give me a job, but he was happy to allow me to continue as a permanent freelancer, reporting for duty on a daily basis. 'You'll have to sing for your supper, ladeee,' offered Peter.

So I did. Peter was and is a brilliant journalist, with a gift for mentally walking around big stories and seeing them from a different and unique perspective. No respecter of wealth or political power and an enemy of pomposity and false grandeur, Peter naturally attracted the fury of establishment figures during his stewardship of Londoner's Diary.

So laden was his desk with threatened legal actions that he used to jokingly lift the ringing telephone and declare, 'Hello, Londoner's Apology here.'

And he was mischievous. After it was disclosed that one of the Brink's-Mat bullion robbers had been stepping out with a girl who worked in the Harrods perfumery department, Peter came out of the daily news conference with editor Leese and declared, 'The editor would like a reassuring figure to pop down to the Harrods perfume hall and ask if any of the lasses are on the game. McEntee, you are the perfect choice.'

Cue Peter's explosive cackle.

There had been an earlier allegation that some of the females serving rich Arabs in the Knightsbridge emporium had been scribbling their private telephone numbers on the back of receipts for jumbo quantities of Chanel and other pricey unguents.

It was the age before mobile telephones and Leveson, so I wandered the perfume halls accepting sprayed samples of expensive scents, purchasing some small quantities of aftershave and cunningly chatting to the girls about hypothetical dates with high-rolling customers.

There had been much coverage in the newspapers that morning about the Harrods lover of the bullion thief, so it was an easy subject to converse about. It never crossed my mind to reveal to these attractive and delightful women that I was a reporter from the *Evening Standard* just up the road in Kensington.

I telephoned the *Standard*, asked for copy and dictated what I thought was a witty and diverting 600 words for the Diary. In conclusion, I asked to speak to McKay. After quickly reading the copy, he asked 'What about names? We need the girls' names.'

Shamefully, I returned to the perfume hall and discreetly jotted down the names of my informants from the badges they wore, Mandy from Chanel, Tricia from Burberry and so on. I added the names to the copy.

After my offering appeared that afternoon, I received a telephone call. 'Hello, I'm Ann. I work for Lancôme in Harrods. Are you the man I sold some perfume to this morning after we chatted about the Brink's-Mat girl?' I said I was. 'Well, we've all been fired. I've been told to leave Harrods immediately. So have the other girls. I am a single mother. I can't afford to lose this job. What are you going to do about it?' She was weeping.

I was appalled. I was explaining the development to Peter when he got an urgent call from Brian Vine, the managing editor of the *Daily Mail*, then owners of the *Standard*, and a friend of Harrods' proprietor Mohamed Al-Fayed.

Vine was furious. Not about the sacking of my friends from the perfumery department, but the sudden and immediate withdrawal of Harrods' multimillion-pound advertising revenue as a result of the piece in Londoner's Diary – from not only the *Standard*, but also the mother title, the *Daily Mail*.

Vine asked to speak to me. Recollection of the expletive-riddled bollocking he delivered still gives me goose bumps (of course, the indestructible McKay went on to accept Mohamed's invitation to lose £10 million as the re-launch editor of *Punch* magazine).

Peter also dispatched me to the St Bride's memorial

service for the wife of *Express* proprietor Lord Stevens. She had choked on a peach and the *Daily Telegraph*, without a prepared obituary, quoted at length from a book she'd written about how to please the man in your life. The forensic description of the lost art of toe sucking carried by the *Telegraph* so enraged Stevens he threatened to pull the *Express* out of a proposed Docklands publishing venture with the *Telegraph*.

'Ask Lord Stevens what he thinks of today's *Telegraph* obituary,' declared Peter, as if he were sending me off to a Downing Street briefing with the PM. As soon as I arrived at the back door of St Bride's, I spotted the garlanded coffin in front of the altar. It wasn't a memorial service, it was the funeral of Lady Stevens.

Like the Vine bollocking, I hesitate to recollect the reaction of Lord Stevens as I reached the head of the queue of consoling mourners, just as his wife's coffin was borne shoulder-high from the church directly behind him. Will 'how dare you' do?

Peter McKay found this hilarious. A few weeks later, the declaration of the Ayatollah Khomeini's obscene fatwa on Salman Rushdie for having the impertinence to write *The Satanic Verses* coincided with another of Peter's story ideas. 'We've been invited to have tea with Britt Ekland at the Cumberland Hotel about her forthcoming appearance in pantomime,' explained Peter. 'Go and ask her what she thinks of the Iranian fatwa.'

Off I went. Over Earl Grey with the still handsome ex-wife of Peter Sellers, I mentioned the Ayatollah Khomeini. 'Who?' asked the Swedish firecracker. I explained that Mr Rushdie had just gone into hiding as a result of the threat from Khomeini to have him killed.

Had she a message for the Ayatollah? Britt carefully placed her teacup back in its saucer on the coffee table in her suite and clenched her first. 'If the Ayatollah Khomeini were here I would punch him on the nose.'

Peter transformed my few pedestrian paragraphs into a sombre warning to the Iranian leader from Miss Britt Ekland, the well-known actress who was about to appear in *Jack and the Beanstalk* at the Theatre Royal Windsor.

There was a postscript. Miss Ekland telephoned to thank me for the piece. 'At last,' she gushed, 'someone has taken me seriously!'

While very much enjoying my stint on McKay's Diary, I was still a freelancer with a wife, two very young children and a big mortgage to support. But Jeffrey Archer was about to inadvertently provide secure employment for the Chancer from Cavan.

During my Londoner's Diary sojourn, Jeffrey was

deputy chairman of the Conservative Party. He fervently believed that one day he would be Prime Minister.

It was 1988 and I had gate-crashed a soirée at the private residence of the Irish ambassador Andy O'Rourke, located above the first-floor ballroom at the palatial embassy in Belgravia.

It was to celebrate the life of Seán O'Casey's widow, Eileen. She was there and most of the attendees were from the book trade.

Unexpectedly, Archer bounded in. I asked him why he had turned up. 'Seán O'Casey is my favourite author,' he replied brazenly. I then asked if he still had ambitions to be Prime Minister.

Loudly he proclaimed, 'Of course I want to be the Prime Minister.' Within earshot was Aileen MacGowran, widow of the great Beckett actor Jack MacGowran (he also played the film director in the original film of *The Exorcist*).

She theatrically placed her right palm on her forehead and declared loudly, 'Oh, what humility!' This infuriated Archer. He immediately pinned Aileen to the nearby wall and lectured her. 'OK, so what is wrong with wanting to be *Prime Minister*? If I said I wanted to be a doorman at the Irish embassy, would that be okay?' A member of the embassy staff intervened and calmed Jeffrey down. He flounced out.

Naturally, the following morning I wrote up the incident for Londoner's Diary. It was the lead story under the headline: 'Jeffrey loses his sense of humour at the Irish embassy'. By lunchtime, the editor of the *Standard*, the late John Leese, had received a hand-delivered letter from the Irish ambassador complaining about my attendance at his home the previous evening.

It stated, 'While we are always delighted to see members of the *Evening Standard* staff at our Embassy, on this occasion Mr John McEntee was not invited.' The ambassador's complaint, designed to cause me trouble at the *Standard*, was prompted by Archer's complaint to the embassy. I was called in by Leese, who asked me what my circumstances were.

I told him I was freelancing. A short time later, I was given a staff job. While I owe the start of my illustrious career on the *Standard* to Lord Archer, there was a downside. I was barred from all further embassy functions – St Patrick's Day, the visit of various Presidents and Taoiseachs and the famous Christmas party where, long after my exclusion, a homeward-bound and well-refreshed cleric clambered into the back of someone else's car and declared, 'I'm the Bishop of Southwark. 'Tis what I do.'

Eventually I was restored to favour, and the embassy's excellent draught Guinness, by a new envoy, Ted Barrington.

Later that summer I motored to Cambridge with my wife Colette, then pregnant with our third child Jack, to raise a glass with Archer's wife Mary to celebrate the publication of a privately published volume about poet Rupert Brooke, a previous occupant of the Archers' Grantchester home.

Jeffrey was at that time assiduously touring the country buttering up constituency workers in his role as fundraiser and morale-booster for the Tory Party. Mary had chosen one such occasion when Jeffrey was safely away campaigning in the West Country to have a media tea party in the spacious garden, which meandered to the banks of the Cam.

It was a glorious late summer day at the beautiful house where the words 'Stands the clock at five to three / Is there still honey for tea?' originated.

It wasn't long after three that we heard the scrunch of tyres on the gravel drive. Jeffrey had raced back for the launch. The look on Mary Archer's face said it all. She was deeply unhappy at what she saw as her husband's upstaging of the event.

Most of us abandoned Mary and gravitated towards Jeffrey. He was wearing a straw boater and striped blazer and spouting about his plans for the country. He produced a painting wrapped in brown paper, stood on a chair and announced that he had a surprise present for his darling wife. Mary looked bemused, tore open the gift, glanced briefly at it before placing it carelessly on the lawn. Shortly afterwards, she was posing on a bench for the local photographer clutching a copy of the book when Jeffrey appeared behind her doing Frankie Vaughan-style high kicks and waving his hat about. Mrs Archer, as she was then, turned around and mouthed the words 'fuck off' before resuming her smile for the camera.

In the Fleet Street of the '70s and '80s, afternoons were invariably spent in Vagabonds, a drinking club in Fetter Lane run by a defrocked Scotland Yard policeman from County Fermanagh. At the time, the pubs closed between 3 p.m. and 5 p.m. and a honeycomb of drinking clubs did a roaring business. Vagabonds had no windows and no clocks and when hacks stayed too long, complimentary oysters and sausages were served by big-breasted barmaids to keep the customers from going to restaurants elsewhere.

My regular drinking companion was JAK, aka Raymond Jackson, the *Evening Standard* cartoonist (the *Standard* was still in the black-glassed *Express* building in Fleet Street).

JAK was so valued by the *Standard* that he could afford, on expenses, to have a permanent minicab at his disposal, ferrying him everywhere, with the hapless driver having to while away endless hours on the pavement while he indulged his passion for talk, champagne and girls.

This particular afternoon, JAK and I adjourned from Vagabonds and motored to Soho, where we climbed the rickety stairs to the Colony Room in Dean Street.

Muriel Belcher was not long dead and Ian Board, known as IDA, who possessed an enormous throbbing nose, was hunched behind the bar.

When we arrived, the artist Francis Bacon, in a full-length, brown leather coat, was drinking champagne with his young boyfriend John Edwards.

Nearby in an alcove was a very drunk Patrick Conyngham, younger brother of Lord Henry Mountcharles, who organised rock concerts in his front garden at Slane Castle in Ireland.

Patrick, a dissolute figure, was known for some reason as 'the Underwater Poet'.

Various thirsty regulars were sitting and standing just outside Bacon's orbit watching developments like hawks. Francis embraced JAK warmly and then beckoned the barman to open another bottle of champagne.

His mantra was: 'Here is champagne for my real friends, and real pain for my sham friends.' Bacon thrust his hand into his coat pocket and produced a rolled-up wad of notes.

They were twenties. I calculated that he had about £1,000 in his stash, a considerable sum then. As the champagne appeared, the motley collection of freeloaders, like jackals around a campfire, edged closer to our company in the hope of a glass of fizzy.

Bacon curtly told them to fuck off. John Edwards, in slacks and a sweater with a long college scarf around his neck and hanging down his front, was perched on a stool. Unaware that he was Bacon's lover, I asked him what he did for a living. 'I'm a photographer,' he replied haughtily.

I asked what he photographed: 'Just Francis,' he snapped. 'Do you have your own darkroom?' He looked at me curiously and replied, 'No, I take my film to Boots.' Hardly Don McCullin.

He subsequently inherited Bacon's money and works of art and went off to live in Thailand with an East End thug who was his boyfriend. Edwards died prematurely, leaving all of the great painter's work to his oafish boyfriend. He too is now dead.

Before leaving the Colony Room with JAK, I asked Bacon to autograph a cheque in my Allied Irish Bank book. He scrawled his signature. But then my cartoonist friend spoiled it by insisting on writing 'JAK' underneath.

It was during this period I became friendly with Jilly Cooper. It was before her huge success as a novelist with *Riders* and *Polo* and *The Man Who Made Husbands Jealous*. She had just been employed by the Irish Tourist Board to promote the Emerald Isle. Along with the late Robert Morley, she was used in a campaign to highlight the quixotic charms of my native heath. You know the sort of thing: road signs pointing in different directions to the same location. Very 'top o' the mornin', begorrah' kind of stuff.

Jilly was the undoubted star of the campaign. I met her in her husband Leo's attic-like office near Shaftesbury Avenue. Jilly and I had met before and got on well.

She was very flirtatious. Leo pretended to busy himself at his desk while we chatted on a sofa over a glass of wine. Jilly, in all her innocence, made some critical remarks about the Irish climate. I confess that I had started it by saying Ireland was a wonderful country but it needed a roof. How Jilly laughed.

As I scribbled in my notebook, the cannier Leo interjected: 'Darling, do you think you should be saying these things about Ireland?'

Jilly, as much to show her independence from Leo as anything else, proceeded to give me reams and reams of useable copy. It duly appeared in my Dublin-based newspaper.

Shortly afterwards, Jilly's charming endorsement of Ireland was terminated.

To her credit, Jilly didn't hold me responsible and not only gave me a flattering namecheck in her novel *Pandora* but every year since sends me a monogrammed chocolate Advent calendar.

I visited her and Leo for lunch in a pub in the lovely Cotswold village where she still lives and writes. It was a year before poor Leo died from Parkinson's disease in December 2013.

He was cantankerous and difficult, which was under-standable as he had lost his mobility and independence. In an effort to cheer proceedings, I told Jilly about my recent experience in the Dawes Road branch of William Hill, the bookmaker. At the time I was divorced and liv-ing with my partner Morven Fraser in a rented house nearby. We had two pugs, beige Bertie and black Mabel.

During their evening walk, I was in the habit of bring-ing them to Hill's, where I would place a few wagers and Bertie and Mabel could bark at the horses on the big screen.

This particular summer evening I had placed a bet on champion jockey Tony McCoy's nag in the 7.30 race from Market Rasen.

As I watched the race live on the big screen with

another Irishman and two West Indian punters in the shop, Mabel barked ferociously. I assumed it was at the horses but she was looking the other way. Without turning around, I nudged her with my foot and told her to shut up.

She persisted in barking. To my pleasure, McCoy steered his horse to victory. I had won £60. I turned around and presented my winning slip at the counter. The bespectacled twenty-something in the blue William Hill shirt was visibly shaking. 'I ha, ha, haven't any money,' he stuttered. 'What?!' I exclaimed. 'We've just had an armed robbery,' he answered. 'The till is empty.'

Within minutes, a police car screeched to a halt outside the betting emporium. Two uniformed officers entered. The cashier explained what had happened as one of the officers asked myself and the three other customers if we'd seen anything. 'No,' was the universal answer.

We were then invited to view the CCTV footage. The footage showed Mabel barking at a hooded figure brandishing a sawn-off shotgun. He had entered the shop immediately behind myself and the other gamblers, just as the two-mile Market Rasen steeple chase began on the TV screen. We had our backs to him and never noticed his entrance.

He pointed the gun at the terrified cashier and pushed

over a note. It stated: 'Give me all your money or I will shoot you or one of your customers.'

The terrified lad quickly handed over £300 in notes. The gunman was gone before McCoy had reached the winning post. In freeze frame, it was a curious tableau: gamblers watching a race, dog barking, man with gun standing behind.

A policewoman then arrived with printed forms. 'Does anyone require counselling?' she asked. One of my West Indian friends quipped, 'No, but if you have a tip for the 8 o'clock at Market Rasen that would be handy.'

In her forthcoming book, Jilly has used the story but turned dear Mabel into a Labrador.

Fleet Street in the '70s and '80s nurtured a heavy drinking culture. One afternoon, the legendary *Daily Express* journalist Brian Vine was hurrying from his office along Fleet Street to El Vino, located near the Law Courts, when he was accosted by a friend on the pavement. Brian's response: 'Sorry, old boy. Can't stop, I'm in a taxi.' Flann O'Brien was alive and well in Vine.

I used to frequent the Tipperary, a long, narrow bar that was originally a Mooney's pub. At the time, *The Sun* and the *News of the World* were printed on giant presses in Bouverie Street just around the corner from the Tipp. Most lunchtimes, about a dozen of the News International printers and electricians in their trademark overalls would trudge in and take up residence. Feet across the space between their bar stools and the bar, they were a nuisance, demanding kisses from female customers for free passage to the toilets. But the manager, Tom from County Clare, recognised their value. 'Some lunchtimes they drink more than a dozen pints of Light and Bitter,' he told me.

This amount of drinking frequently led to wildcat stoppages of the giant printing presses as one or two inebriated operatives fell over in the print hall or caused disruption. As *The Sun* then didn't have any regional printing centre – the presses would start rolling out the Scottish edition mid-afternoon and had to produce nearly 4 million copies – this was disastrous.

Negotiations would take place swiftly and the light-headed Tipperary customer would receive an apology and printing would resume. It was disgraceful and went on until Murdoch absconded to Wapping in 1987.

But, eventually, even Tom the Tipperary host had enough of the bad behaviour of the Bouverie Street boozers. After a week without their presence in the bar, I asked Tom what had occurred. 'I used to pour a generous three-quarter of a pint measure of bitter to mix with their light ales. I dropped the plimsoll line to exactly half a pint and they were off.'

Infrequently I would be joined by the great Maeve Binchy, then the *Irish Times* correspondent, in the Reuters building next door to the *Irish Press*. Maeve liked a drink and when she became famous after the huge success of her debut novel *Light a Penny Candle* a publicist confided that on book tours 'Maeve gets very tetchy if she hasn't a gin and tonic in her hand by noon'.

Despite this, she was a wonderful journalist with an enviable, accessible skill. Meeting her regularly on various jobs, I had no idea she was rising pre-dawn to write novels.

Often we would meet in hotels as she finished interviewing someone (Ed McBain, Iris Murdoch, Paul Newman) and I was about to take my turn for the regulation sound-bite controlled by the publicists. We enjoyed raising many a glass in the King & Keys or in the Italian restaurant next door. Highly disciplined, she rose at 5 a.m. and worked on her manuscript before making the journey from her tiny house in Olympia to Fleet Street.

She always mocked herself and even when the book was taking off joked about an encounter in a Nottingham radio station. She was there to talk about her book, a subject the harassed presenter hadn't a clue about.

She was ushered to her seat during a commercial break and when they went live on air the DJ asked, 'Now, tell me, Miss Binchy, how long have you been making your own furniture?'

Later she and her devoted husband Gordon Snell moved back to Dalkey in south Dublin and made less frequent forays to London. I knew that she was waiting to have hips replaced and approached the operation with some trepidation. At a do in the Irish embassy I spotted her beaming and resplendent, standing in the middle of the ballroom floor in a magnificent flowing dress that reached her ankles. 'So, you've had your hips done?' I asked. 'Not yet,' she chuckled, beckoning my gaze downward as she lifted her voluminous skirt to show that she was sitting on a shooting stick with a rubber tip.

Maeve was remarkably and discreetly generous. When *Irish Times* colleague James Downey was returning to Dublin, she organised a farewell lunch upstairs at Manzi's fish restaurant off Leicester Square. Like a lady in a local bingo hall doorway, Maeve sat demanding our £10 contribution to the lunch. It was only as the tenth bottle of Frascati whizzed up the table that the penny dropped. There was no way this lunch could be covered by our meagre contribution of £10 a head. It cost nearly £1,000. Maeve discreetly picked up the bill. While she had recently become a millionaire on her book royalties, it was still a lovely gesture.

Through a number of incarnations I had the pleasure of interviewing Anthony Burgess. I always found him helpful, gossipy and full of fun. On the day his book *Earthly Powers* lost out to William Golding's novel for the Booker Prize I was with him at the Connaught Hotel. He had so infuriated his Italian-born wife she chased him around the suite with a poker. In the late '80s he sanctioned a disastrous musical version of *A Clockwork Orange*, staged at the Barbican. As few people had had a chance to see the movie version starring Malcolm McDowell, it was an ambitious project. The music was written by a then little-known Irish group called U2. On the press night, the production was deemed to be dire. Bono, The Edge and the other two members of U2 turned up with their manager Paul McGuinness and publicly endorsed the show (they would, wouldn't they?). I encountered Burgess in the interval and, knowing that he fancied himself as a composer, asked him what he thought of U2's compositions for his book. He was scathing: slagging off the rhythm, style and beat. I duly wrote up Tony's criticisms for the Londoner's Diary on the *Evening Standard*.

Burgess was furious. By lunchtime, a fax had arrived

for editor John Leese saying he had been gulled into saying things he hadn't meant to say by a Hibernian rogue, namely me. We never did get a chance to make it up before his unexpected and untimely death.

When Rory Knight Bruce was appointed editor of Londoner's Diary, I found it sensible to depart. Rory had brought in a chum, a serving British Army officer, Marcus Scriven, to do shifts on the Diary. I asked Marcus if he could get me a few shifts with the British Army on the Rhine. 'Not with your accent,' he joked. Scriven was appointed deputy when I left for *The Times*.

PART 4

GOSSIP AND BLARNEY

There followed a far from happy year as deputy diary editor at *The Times* under Nigel Williamson, a pimply little man with large spectacles who had less charisma than a bunch of nettles. He took exception when he discovered that our principal freelance contributor was a made-up name and I was actually providing the stories. Instead of wondering at my output, he asked me to resign. Years later, flying high as William Hickey, I ignored him on the South Bank. He responded with a nasty fax to the William Hickey desk alerting anyone who bothered to read it of my earth-shattering fiddle. I was reminded of our first meeting at El Vino when he hired me. 'John,' he lisped. 'It will be fun, fun, fun.' No, Nigel, it was 'shit, shit, shit'.

Unlike the sequel to my curious evening with Caroline Aherne at the Groucho (described earlier in the introduction to this book). The afternoon after my abrupt dismissal, my mobile telephone trilled. I answered it.

'Hi, it's Caroline,' came a very small, faraway voice. 'Caroline who?' I asked. 'Caroline Aherne ... I'm sorry for what happened last night. Jaci says you are a really nice guy. Is there any way I can make it up to you?' I seized the opportunity. 'Will you be the guest of honour at my National Treasures lunch next Tuesday?' She readily agreed. Result! And, not only did she turn up at the lunch table, she brought Craig Cash with her.

She was charm itself. It was shortly after her so-called suicide bid and her stint of rehabilitation at the Priory. She told me that when she was discharged from rehab she cannily agreed to a picture spread and interview in the feel-good magazine *Hello!* accompanied by her mother and grandmother – a native of Gort in County Galway. Posing for pictures on a Manchester hotel sofa, she had creased up when her granny whispered from behind her rictus smile: 'Tell me, Caroline, what made you take to the drink?'

It was a successful lunch, memorable for the unexpected arrival of Denis Thatcher, husband of Margaret.

I had, tongue in cheek, sent an invitation to Mrs Thatcher and wasn't surprised when I didn't receive a reply.

Denis had clearly accepted on her behalf but neglected to RSVP. He asked for a gin martini and we rearranged the chairs to make room for him. Refreshed with three jumbo gins, he was firing on all cylinders, even making a short, witty 'thank you' speech at the end.

After the lunch, I flicked through our visitors' book to find the following message in elegant copperplate: 'Dear John, Thank you so much for a delightful lunch and I am so sorry my wife Margaret fucked up the country. Denis (Thatcher).'

My amazement quickly vanished when I realised the message was in the same handwriting as an equally effusive message on the previous page, signed by Caroline Aherne. I mentioned Caroline's prank to my friend Peter McKay, author of the mischievous Ephraim Hardcastle column in the *Daily Mail*. He wrote a funny piece about it.

The following week, at a drinks party in Hatchards book shop in Piccadilly, I was approached by an irate Denis Thatcher. Pointing a finger, he snapped: 'Treachery! Treachery!' No fool he.

Denis was terrific company, enjoyed a drink and clearly adored not only his wife Margaret but their daughter Carol. She was, and remains, a jolly-hockey-sticks type but, alas, was unlucky in God's queue for beauty and femininity – she got the orange juice.

In 2005, she triumphed in the down-market reality show *I'm a Celebrity ... Get Me Out of Here!*. I had a hunch she would win and had £20 on her at fourteen to one. When she won I shouted at the TV, 'Weighed in! Weighed in!'

At the time I was working as a gossip columnist on the *Daily Mail* and a girl I knew who subbed on Richard Ingrams's *Oldie* magazine tipped me off that the following week Ingrams would anoint Carol – then aged fifty-three – as Oldie of the Year at his magazine's annual awards lunch at Simpson's-in-the-Strand.

I called Carol to congratulate her (in reality to confirm the tip and write the scoop). She gushed her delight excitedly down the telephone. I duly wrote it up. As a result of the paragraph, Carol was asked by the *Mail* to write a page feature about how thrilled she was to be following in the footsteps of her late father Denis, who had been a previous Oldie of the Year.

It appeared the day before the *Oldie* awards were announced. I went to the lunch – berthing beforehand at the adjacent Coal Hole pub on the Strand for a livener.

Richard very decently seated me at the top table in a love sandwich between two chums, Dame Beryl

Bainbridge and novelist Jilly Cooper. Over the steak and kidney pudding, Jilly dropped a bombshell. She had travelled from her home in Gloucestershire to accept the Oldie of the Year award on behalf of her pal Camilla Parker Bowles, now the Duchess of Cornwall and married to Prince Charles, the heir to the throne.

Carol Thatcher, seated further along the table in front of a packed assembly of crinklies and wrinklies, was preening herself in expectation of Ingrams's imminent announcement of her triumph.

In reality, she had been selected for the lesser accolade of Old Trout of the Year. *Que?* Then the penny dropped. When I had called Carol a few days before to congratulate her, she wrongly assumed I was confirming that she had won. I had, simultaneously, erroneously assumed that she was actually confirming my tip. Crikey!

I reached for the bottle of Chablis at Beryl's elbow and poured myself a bracing top-up, waiting for Richard to clear his throat and expose my gaffe.

Mercifully, when he did rise to his feet, he confirmed my scoop by announcing Carol as a worthy winner. Camilla, in absentia, got Old Trout of the Year. Pondering the power of the *Daily Mail*, I thought there's a higher truth than fact.

Dear Beryl was a regular at the *Oldie* lunches, as well

as gracing my National Treasure feasts. She was also the *Oldie* magazine's drama critic, once going to the wrong West End theatre but cheerfully reviewing the play anyway.

Shortly after the *Oldie* lunch we bumped into each other in the throng at the Author of the Year party among the groaning bookshelves of Hatchards on Piccadilly.

During our natter, there was a fuss at the front door as former PM John Major arrived with his wife Norma. Beryl and I had been great friends with John's pooter-ish brother Terry Major-Ball, a wonderful source of gossip about the PM and an ongoing embarrassment to his younger brother. He had, inevitably, slipped into obscurity after John lost the 1997 general election to Tony Blair.

'I'll ask him about Terry,' I whispered to Beryl, slipping away to introduce myself to the former Tory PM. 'How is Terry?' I asked. John blinked and pushed his glasses back up his nose. 'Haven't you heard?' he replied brusquely. 'Terry is dead!' Norma nodded forlornly as John added, 'He died two months ago.' He explained that Terry had moved from Croydon to the coast, where he had passed away. As I mumbled sympathy, the tiny figure of Beryl, a brimming glass of Pinot Grigio clutched in her right hand, lurched into view. She peered up at Major and asked, 'How is Terry?' John looked at Beryl, looked at me and then, turning to Norma, bleated in that squeaky schoolboy voice, 'There's two of them!'

I was very fond of Beryl. A brilliant writer, she loved a fag. When she gave up tobacco her prodigious literary output ground to a halt. She got writer's block. She liked a drink and I am still amazed at how prolific she was despite her alcohol intake. She told me she didn't trust banks and had hidden her cash royalties in a series of metal cylinders in her Kentish Town garden. (I wonder if the loot is still there?)

At one of my lunches, she brilliantly put Dame Joan Collins in her place. It was a pre-Christmas get-together. In keeping with the season, I'd pushed the boat out with a selection of £6 crackers from Harvey Nichols. You know the sort of thing – braided paper, containing a substantial geegaw jewellery, hair clip, nail cutters.

A cracker was placed with the cutlery at each place setting and half a dozen formed a pyramid in the centre of the table. Beryl sat between Sir Peter O' Sullevan, the famous 'Voice of Racing' and *Oh, Brother!* star Derek Nimmo. I sat opposite, between Joan Collins and Melvyn Bragg. Joan looked ravishing, though I noticed that when she turned to speak to me at the table her hair followed a millisecond after.

As I rose on my hind legs to welcome the guests,

there was a sharp crack as Joan turned to Melvyn and pulled the first cracker. She then asked fellow guest Sue MacGregor to pull another cracker. She opened her small designer handbag and popped the plunder from both crackers into the bag.

By the time I sat down, Joan had completed a scorched-earth policy in relation to the available crackers. But she wasn't quite finished. 'John,' she mewled, 'be a darling and pass me those crackers in the middle of the table.'

What could I do? I got up again and leaned over to harvest the crackers. Before I could hand them to Joan, the diminutive, black-clad figure of Beryl Bainbridge dashed from the other side of the table and squeezed herself between the seated Joan and myself. 'Can I have those crackers for my grandchildren?' she asked. Flummoxed, I didn't reply. Joan, still seated, raised her head and fluttered her eyelashes. 'But, Beryl, I just loooove Christmas crackers.'

Beryl simply grabbed the crackers and clutched them to her bosom, saying, 'But, Joanie, these are for *my* grandchildren. You must understand … you're a granny too.'

Joan didn't bear any grudge. However, afterwards we fell out when I published a paragraph in my Wicked Whispers column in the *Daily Mail* revealing her abhorrence of Birmingham. She'd been touring with a play co-starring the likeable *Brideshead Revisited* actor Nickolas Grace.

She had revealed her feelings on Brum to Nickolas, who had naively confided to someone who worked for me. When her views appeared in a gossip column, Nickolas was mortified. While the tale was true, Nickolas got it in the neck from Joan, who was then sojourning in New York with young husband Percy Gibson. She demanded a retraction. I resisted, but poor Nickolas was caught between a rock and a hard place. He pleaded with me. Eventually it was agreed that Joan would send a fax from New York with a form of words that might allow us to print something without actually saying sorry. In the end, her fax was so funny it went in unaltered. She concluded by saying, 'I love Birmingham and the people of Birmingham. Thanks to you I cannot return there without running the risk of being lynched.' What a gal!

The antics of Joan and Beryl at that particular lunch, however, were totally overshadowed by what happened to fellow guest Derek Nimmo after the meal. Derek had just returned from a Middle East tour of Ray Cooney's farce *Run for Your Wife*. Poignantly, he had prepared a speech and was quite crestfallen when I whispered in his ear that there were no speakers, just eating, drinking and gossiping.

After Joan and other guests had gone, he lingered over the Châteauneuf-de-Pape with Sir Peter, retired sports presenter Dickie Davies and Beryl.

As the clock edged towards 4.30 I mumbled apologies about having to return to work. I accompanied the well-refreshed quartet to the sixth-floor lift and their waiting limousines parked outside the building on Blackfriars Bridge Road. I remember waving Derek off.

The following morning I was summoned to Rosie Boycott's office and asked, 'What did you do to Derek Nimmo?'

I shrugged my shoulders and replied, 'Nothing, Rosie.'

'He is in hospital,' she explained. 'He is in a coma. He fell down a flight of stairs.'

I blinked and did a mental re-run. No, we didn't use the stairs. Yes, I saw him to his car and, no, there was no stumble before he was engulfed by the back door of the limousine.

Word spread quickly. The gossip on the Fleet Street grapevine was that I was responsible for Derek's unfortunate accident. I had forced drink on him, he'd got up from the table, somehow fell down the stairs and that was that.

But, while Derek might have consumed his own body weight in claret, he didn't seem particularly inebriated when I bade him farewell after what was a splendidly well-watered repast.

Now the *Gas and Gaiters* star was unable to speak.

What happened? Here is the truth as I've pieced it together. Instead of pointing his driver in the direction of his Kensington home, Derek gave instructions to head for his beloved Garrick Club. Champagne was consumed before he finally chartered a course for home. There he hardly had time to throw water on his face before he was off to dinner with his beloved wife Patricia. It was after dinner, arriving at his front door of his home, that dear Derek met his fate. Checking an outside fire alarm, he stumbled, fell and hit his head on the outside stone basement stairs. He lingered for two months before dying without regaining consciousness.

After Derek's death in February 1999, his wife asked if she could visit the boardroom where Derek enjoyed his last lunch. I took her around the room, showing her where Derek sat and recalling the happy event. 'He was in fine form,' I explained, mentioning his undelivered speech. In tears she told me, 'He really enjoyed being here.'

I attended his memorial service at the Actors' Church St Paul's in Covent Garden. After the service, I queued with other mourners to pay my respects to his widow.

Patricia was standing outside the church on the top step of the pillared entrance. When I finally arrived at the head of the queue, Patricia greeted me warmly. She stepped back and lost her balance. Her high heel scrunched through the decaying cement on the top step. I grabbed her by the waist to prevent her falling. One of the photographers watching from the bottom of the steps yelled, 'You're not going to kill her as well!'

Derek's tragic demise was the latest episode in a ghoulish pattern that marked a substantial chunk of my professional life. Many people, mostly celebrities, who came into contact with me soon shuffled off their mortal coils. (It began in 1974 with the demise of Ireland's oldest man, Jeremiah McCarthy.)

In 2013, the June edition of the *Oldie* magazine carried my interview with the former British heavyweight boxer Henry Cooper. A cartoon of Henry filled the front cover. The interview inside was in the magazine's 'Still With Us' section. Sadly, however, Henry was in fact no longer still with us. He had taken the celestial final count just as the magazine was going to press. It prompted *Oldie* editor Richard Ingrams to tell the *London Evening Standard*: 'It's the curse of McEntee. He once killed the oldest man in Ireland.'

An early manifestation of my unfortunate gift occurred

when, as a junior reporter on a Dublin newspaper, I had breakfast with Hollywood star John Wayne in the Gresham Hotel.

He was filming the cop movie *Brannigan* in London and had flown over to see his old friend Lord Killanin, who had worked with him on John Ford's *The Quiet Man* in the '50s.

At the time, John was in remission from cancer, what he called 'The Big C'. Within months of our breaking croissants together, the disease returned and he was dead.

A few years later and living in London, I took tea with James Stewart at Claridge's. He was promoting a new print of *The Philadelphia Story*. Though elderly and frail, he was in good shape. After we said cheerio, he was gone to join his chum Mr Wayne within six months.

Bette Davis also granted me an audience at Claridge's and was featured in the obituary pages soon after.

A seemingly fit Lee Marvin was in London to talk about his part in the Russian thriller *Gorky Park*. We had a tremendously enjoyable conversation where he revealed that he had had the pleasure of killing Ronald Reagan in a B movie in which Ronald had played an IRA terrorist. Result? The following year, Lee succumbed to the lung ailment that had prompted him to move to the arid joys of Arizona.

Need I go on? Kenneth More slipped away prematurely after we'd met at the St George's Hotel off Oxford Street to talk about his autobiography. Eamonn Andrews seemed in good form when we met at his Chiswick flat. No sooner had I received a letter inviting me to a recording of *This Is Your Life* than Eamonn was gone. Peter Cushing didn't last long after I interviewed him in Brown's Hotel. Kenneth Tynan's gorgeous wife Kathleen insisted she was in fine fettle but died within weeks of our cosy chat at her book launch in Lord Weidenfeld's palatial Chelsea flat. (In mitigation, I shook hands with George Weidenfeld and he lived to the grand old age of ninety-six before joining Mrs Tynan in 2016.)

I even had the cheek over a fish lunch at Manzi's much-missed restaurant off Leicester Square to ask *Yes, Minister* and *The Good Life* star Paul Eddington if the rumours about his ill health were true. The handwritten letter he wrote insisting his doctors had told him he would live into his eighth decade arrived the week his death was on the TV news.

When I finally pop my clogs, I hope my tombstone doesn't read 'The Man Who Killed Derek Nimmo'.

At least Sir Kingsley Amis was immune from The Curse of McEntee. When we first met in the mid-'70s, he was in his prime.

But his drinking was heroic; his permanent thirst assuaged by substantial quantities of free booze provided by the *Daily Express*, where he wrote a weekly column about alcohol. (One of his memorable tips to save on gin at parties was to dip a finger in the bottle and run it around the rim of the glass, then fill it with diluted gin supplemented with ice and lemon. The recipient usually recoiled as his or her lips came in contact with the undiluted spirit at the top of the glass.)

His column prompted a small book, *Everyday Drinking*. His publisher arranged for us to meet to talk about the book in El Vino, the journalist's Fleet Street watering hole. At the time I was a fallow twenty-three, naive and with a modest salary that didn't stretch to expenses for entertaining famous authors – or unknowns for that matter.

I soon realised that Amis's mission was to get pissed at my expense.

His portly frame buttoned into a dark overcoat, his Lucky Jim good looks faded with bloated features and encroaching baldness, he sat in a leather armchair in the back saloon perusing the El Vino whisky menu. 'I'll have a large Macallan,' he declared in a business-like way, addressing me as a waiter.

I went to the bar and got him his jumbo malt. He said

little. A sniff of the glass, a swift gulp and the beaker was empty.

'I think I'll move on to Glenfiddich,' declared Kingsley as he slid the empty glass in my direction. Glenmorangie followed. And then Macallan. He spent the next hour delivering monosyllabic answers to my questions while working his way through El Vino's extensive and expensive malt repertoire of offerings.

Occasionally he stopped mid gulp, narrowed his eyes, weasel-like, and snapped, 'Remind me of who you are.' But the winning smile reappeared each time I returned with another winking dark distillation from the bogs and glens of Scotland. By now quite drunk, he peered at his watch. 'Good heavens! Is that the time? I'm meeting someone at the Garrick – awfully nice to meet you.' I was left to settle up. The bill was more than my week's wages.

I interviewed him again on the eve of the royal wedding in 1981. Fleet Street was festooned with celebratory bunting as Prince Charles and his new bride Diana Spencer would soon canter in a carriage through the Street of Shame after their marriage in nearby St Paul's Cathedral.

I had taken the precaution this time of asking him to come to our tiny office in Chronicle House opposite the *Daily Telegraph*. He sat forlornly behind my desk answering questions politely about the paperback edition of his novel *Russian Hide and Seek*. He seemed distracted, preoccupied. He then asked plaintively, 'Do you fancy coming to the Garrick for a drink?' I declined – something I now regret.

In 1989, while working for Londoner's Diary on the *Standard*, I telephoned Kingsley to ask if it was true that he had a passion for *Crossroads*, the curious ITV soap opera based in a fictitious Birmingham motel. '*Crossroads*?' he barked. 'Never heard of it. What is it?' I explained. 'No, never watch it,' he said. 'But *Coronation Street*, now you're talking. I love it. Never miss it. That Ken Barlow is a one eh? Ha ha.'

In the subsequent years before his death I encountered Kingsley at drinks parties and signings. His trademark scowl invariably vanished when I mentioned *Coronation Street*. We would bring each other up to speed on the plot and the activities of Deirdre Barlow, barmaid Bet Lynch and the randy Ken. Onlookers assumed we were the best of chums. We weren't, but we had a common interest: *Corrie*.

While not quite meriting inclusion in Kingsley Amis's first eleven of world-class piss artists, Frank Longford enjoyed a drink or two. Frank has been dead for more than a decade now (2001) and I still miss him. He was a diarist's dream: gossipy and indiscreet and never taking offence when I described him frequently in print as the 'delightfully dotty Labour peer Lord Longford'.

He loved lunch and, like interior designer Nicky Haslam, would attend the opening of a wound.

At what turned out to be our last meal at the Gay Hussar in 2001, I arrived after Frank, who was berthed in a banquette. Almost blind and very frail, his alabaster forehead was dotted with three Band Aids covering minor cuts he'd suffered in his numerous falls (he refused to use a stick right up until the tap on the shoulder from the Grim Reaper).

He was peering intently with his sightless eyes across the restaurant at the sound of voices from a distant table. He could hear but not see ex-*Private Eye* editor Richard Ingrams, his successor Ian Hislop and the late Paul Foot settling their bill prior to departure. He asked me who they were. I told him and excused myself to go and wash my hands. When I returned, Frank had shuffled across to where the trio had eaten and was blissfully addressing the empty table.

I led him gently back to his already cut chicken, which the staff had kindly dissected for him. Frank instinctively executed his trademark post-lunch ritual to avoid the bill. Asking the time and getting flustered, he explained he was already late for a vital debate in the House of

Lords. It was a device I was delighted to accept. Alas, it was the last time I saw dear Frank. He was dead within two months. But then, he was ninety-five.

His daughter Lady Antonia Fraser recently published *My History*, a memoir of her early life. The stories of her shambolic father brought back memories of the endearing gift that kept on giving to a gossip columnist like myself.

On one occasion, Frank turned up at the Gay Hussar for lunch with a huge pigeon dropping on his bald dome. No one, including me, had the courage to point out the deposit and he headed off to the House of Lords after lunch still adorned by bird poo. One of our most unforgettable encounters occurred when Frank, then in his seventies, wrote a compendium of accidents suffered by famous people. His own mishap, included in the book, happened in 1946 when, as Labour's Minister for Germany, he flew to Berlin and, exiting the RAF plane, somehow managed to miss the welcoming steps.

As an army band played 'God Save the King', Lord Longford waved from the open door of the aircraft and plunged more than six feet to the tarmac. On his descent, he must have noticed the steps connected to a door further up the aircraft where a guard of honour waited to welcome the government minister.

To talk about the book I went to Frank's handsome

office in Bloomsbury and was ushered to the boardroom, which contained a magnificent twelve-seater mahogany table. Frank was chairman of publishers Sidgwick & Jackson at the time.

Drink featured, as it did in most of our encounters. He asked if I would like a glass of sherry. I said yes, but Frank frowned when he discovered that the decanter on a side table was empty.

Frank pointed out the first-floor window into Museum Street at a branch of Threshers, the wine merchants, below.

Would I mind popping out and buying a bottle of dry sherry? No money changed hands. I bought the sherry and returned to the boardroom.

After we had talked at length about pratfalls and accidents, and effortlessly emptied the bottle of sherry, Frank insisted on demonstrating his keep-fit routine. Despite his advanced years, he boasted of regular jogs in the Sussex countryside near his home. This was in an age before pilates and designer trainers. 'I don't do press-ups,' explained Frank. 'But I do some sit-ups and squats.'

Sitting on the floor, he demonstrated some slow-motion exercises, creakily moving his knees up and down and waving his arms about. Resuming a standing position, he ran on the spot for a few moments. But then, disaster struck. Spreading his arms and legs to show me a particular stretching technique, a new chapter in Lord Longford's Book of Accidents suddenly began.

His left leg became entangled in one of the mahogany chairs. It fell over onto the carpet. As he suspended his helicoptering right arm to grab the chair, he stumbled and fell forward, his stomach coming into contact with the upturned chair.

I rushed to assist and caught his flailing left hand, which knocked me back. I tripped over the neighbouring mahogany chair. Trying to maintain my balance, I fell on top of Lord Longford. The seat had fallen out of the upturned chair. Lord Longford's head now peered out of the space left by the absent cushion. His left leg became entangled in the neighbouring chair where the seat had also dropped out. I lay alongside his lordship in a labyrinth of mahogany. We were stuck. The door opened and the secretary asked, in a matter-of-fact voice, 'Is everything all right?' I got the distinct impression that this was not the first occasion on which she had found her boss acquainting himself with the furniture on the floor of the Sidgwick & Jackson boardroom.

Frank's first close shave with me and a bill was at the rooftop cocktail bar at the St George's Hotel near the BBC's Broadcasting House in Portland Place.

Frank had been spouting on the radio about his new

biography of Kennedy (he also did Nixon, Éamon de Valera and all the saints). As he emerged from the studio, followed by a middle-aged lady who remained silent, he suggested we adjourn to the St George. The lady, who had not been introduced, followed us across the street and into the express lift to the top floor.

As we emerged on the penthouse floor, Frank turned to the woman, blinked a few times and, nudging his glasses back up his nose, asked, 'What are you doing here?' It transpired it was his secretary from Sidgwick & Jackson, who had accompanied him to the BBC for the interview. Frank had forgotten all about her and with a wave of his hand told her to return to his office in Bloomsbury.

As we sat in the lounge, with a stunning view over the rooftops of Oxford Street and beyond, I anxiously eyed the free nuts and listened to the pianist tip-tapping the ivories on a baby grand. Both indicated a level of expense I wasn't prepared for. I had less than a fiver on me and Frank's reputation had gone before him. A white-jacketed waiter approached and asked 'Good morning, gentlemen, what would you like?' 'Do you mind if I have a large schooner of sherry with my coffee?' Frank requested with a glance in my direction. It was 11 a.m. I asked for a glass of tap water. Frank had made short work of the salted peanuts by the time the waiter returned. Ditto with the sherry. He asked for a second schooner. My mental abacus confirmed that I did not have enough money to cover this transaction. The interview went well and was interrupted only when Frank asked, 'Would you mind if I have another sherry? It's rather good here. Will you have one?'

'No, thanks,' I replied, sipping my gratis water as I beckoned to the patrolling waiter. After polishing off the third schooner, Frank asked, 'What time is it?' It was 12.30 p.m. 'Goodness! I'm expected at the House of Lords,' he said. He stood up, we shook hands and he walked towards the express lift. As his tall, gangly figure disappeared, I summoned the waiter to explain my predicament. Before I could open my mouth, he was staring at the leather seat just vacated by his lordship. 'You seem to have dropped some money, sir!' he exclaimed.

There on the green seat was a gleaming hoard of pound coins winking in the midday sun. During our chat, and his heroic consumption of sherry, Frank's pockets had disgorged a total of ten pound coins and some assorted shrapnel in the form of fifty pence pieces. I grandly told the waiter to take what he needed (about £10) and to keep the change.

On that occasion I was not on expenses (and didn't possess a credit card), but all of our subsequent nosebags were covered by various proprietors, from Rupert

Murdoch to Lord Stevens and Lord Rothermere. I never begrudged watering Lord Longford. He was always good company: kind, engaging, witty; his only failing vanity.

All our encounters were Pooterish. In 1986, I interviewed his lovely wife Elizabeth on publication of her splendid memoir *The Pebbled Shore*. Near the conclusion of our chat in the sitting room of her apartment in Flood Street, Chelsea, the door opened and the unmistakable head of Lord Longford peered in. 'John, when you are finished might I have a word?'

I asked Lady Longford to sign my copy of her book and was heading for the door when she stood up, beckoned to a full bottle of sherry on the sideboard and said, 'John, take this.' It was accompanied by two glasses. I turned left and walked the length of the corridor to a single bedroom, where Lord Longford lay sprawled on a Spartan metal-framed bed that would not have looked out of place in an army barracks.

'Oh good,' he exclaimed, his eyes lighting up at sight of the sherry. 'Shut the door and sit down.'

As he poured two large glasses of the ruby wine, he asked me, 'Now what did she say about me? Be honest. I don't mind.'

He took me by surprise. Lady Longford had been complimentary about her husband. I was the one who had drawn her attention to his daftness, as outlined in *Pebbled Shore*.

'She says you are eccentric,' I blurted out, 'and that you couldn't change a light bulb. You had to get the butler to do it when you were at Pakenham Hall in Ireland.'

'Oh dear, oh dear,' mumbled Frank as he sipped his Amontillado. 'Anything else?'

I could only remember references to his clumsiness, heartily greeting his titled Irish brother-in-law with an energetic pat on the back that landed him in his lake. Frank seemed to be taking this news rather badly. He was silent for a long time and then brightened up. 'More sherry?'

We managed to finish the bottle as we talked about his hero Éamon de Valera, Irish rugby, and the imminent demise of the Irish Club in Eaton Square. More than an hour had passed when he asked the time. 'Crikey, I must go to evening Mass at the Brompton Oratory. Would you like to come?' I nodded assent as we left the room and the empty sherry bottle and tip-toed down the corridor, past the closed sitting-room door where Lady Longford sat, and went out into Flood Street. We walked to nearby King's Road and found a bus that would take us to Knightsbridge and evening Mass at the Oratory.

Barry Cryer recently shared his encounter with Frank

on a Central Line tube. Finding themselves sitting next to each other, they chatted amicably and, as Barry alighted at Oxford Circus, Lord Longford also got off the train and accompanied Barry through the station on to the escalator and out into Oxford Circus. It was at this point that Frank stopped, looked around and said, 'Where am I?' Barry told him and he replied, 'Oh dear, I'm not supposed to be here', before turning on his heels and re-entering the station.

Frank received much criticism for his lifelong campaigning for prisoners in general and Moors murderess Myra Hindley in particular. Hindley herself went to her grave furious with Longford for his well-meaning efforts, which ultimately kept the spotlight of attention on her and ensured that she would never be granted parole.

Longford's cousin Ferdinand Mount, in his memoir *Cold Cream*, recalls Lord Longford's glumness when obliged to attend a family wedding on the Isle of Wight. He brightened instantly when he remembered that the island contained two high-security prisons, including Parkhurst. 'I'll go and see Reggie Kray,' he declared, confirming that no journey was entirely wasted. And when the *Daily Telegraph* moved from Fleet Street to Canary Wharf in the late '80s, former editor Bill Deedes quipped, 'The only advantage Canary Wharf has over

Wormwood Scrubs is that Lord Longford will not be visiting us in Canary Wharf.'

I liked Lord Longford immensely and recognised that he was a wonderful source of newspaper stories. Once, in a Lebanese restaurant in Kensington, he whipped a proof copy of his latest volume out of his rucksack and said, 'I am very proud of this. The publishers says it is very good.' On the title page was one word: Humility. (The book also dislodged from the bag a crumpled pair of striped, red-and-white pyjamas, which landed on the floor alongside our food-laden table. Frank looked at the jim-jams, then accusingly at me and asked, 'How did they get there?')

Frank Longford was so much nicer than and supe-rior company to that of his perennially dour son-in-law Harold Pinter, who, Pinteresquely, had ... married ... Frank's daughter ... Lady Antonia. (Pause, sigh, glare, scream.) Following his death in 2012, Antonia wrote a moving memoir entitled *Must You Go?*. After its pub-lication, I encountered her at Random House's annual publishing shindig at the Natural History Museum. I had just arrived and she was collecting her coat and about to depart. 'Must you go?' I asked. Pleased? She wasn't.

I frequently encountered her and 'Arold at book launches, theatre openings and gallery events in London.

Antonia possessed (and still does) that wonderful upper-class ability of being icily polite as she cuts you dead. But at least she was always more civil than 'Arold.

Once, at a literary party, when I asked him about a particular play of his, he declined to answer. Mischievously, I then sought his opinion on the ITV talent show *Pop Idol* – the forerunner to *The X Factor*. He glared at me and boomed, '*Pop Idol*? What is *Pop Idol*?'

As I attempted to explain, he barked, 'I have one word for you.' He then uttered a word that rhymes with 'duck' followed by another word: off. I politely pointed out that, in fact, that was two words. He shouted, 'Antonia, we're leaving', turned on his heel and flounced out followed in hot pursuit by a baffled Lady Antonia.

A few years earlier I attended the West End opening night of a revival of his play *Old Times*, starring Julie Christie. It was mid-winter and I was seated in the Royal Circle directly behind Pinter and Lady Antonia. As the curtain rose on the first act there was some seasonal sneezing and sniffling from the audience. Noses were blown and the coughing was accompanied by the noise of boiled sweets being unwrapped. Pinter was bristling. Ten minutes into the production he rose from his seat, turned his face to the assembled theatregoers and glared. The stage light added menace to his bespectacled eyes. He began his glare at the far right-hand corner of the Royal Circle, sweeping the audience with a withering look of disdain. As he rotated his head towards the middle and then the far left of the auditorium, the sounds of coughing, sniffling and sweet-opening diminished and were replaced with silence. For the rest of that act and the next the audience sat in terror, stifling all noise. He hadn't said a word but it was an impressive performance.

Pinter was never friendly, even scowling menacingly when he spotted me at Lord Longford's ninetieth birthday party in the garden of Frank's East Sussex home. Frank sat with Elizabeth, Denis Healey and Jim Callaghan, a marvellous quartet of dinosaurs in the Sunday afternoon sunshine. Callaghan, thankfully, had forgotten our previous encounter in the Savoy Hotel's river-entrance gentleman's toilet.

It was immediately after *The Spectator*'s annual Parliamentarian of the Year luncheon.

Sunny Jim, then elevated to the House of Lords, had won a gong for his activities on the red benches. It was the late '90s and I was then editor of the newly revived William Hickey column on the *Daily Express*. We happened to find ourselves about to urinate in adjoining traps. But first, some background.

The former Labour Prime Minister had been embarrassed when Francis Wheen's biography of fellow Labour MP Tom Driberg revealed Driberg's admiration for Jim's impressively proportioned penis. Wheen recounted a story about the homosexual Driberg – who was also the first and best William Hickey columnist on Beaverbrook's *Daily Express* – sharing a car journey back from his constituency with Callaghan.

Both men were then ambitious young backbenchers. During the long journey, both men felt the call of nature and pulled up to urinate on the side of the road. As they were doing so, Driberg took a peek at Callaghan's willy and was very impressed with what he saw. He recorded his admiration in his diary. While Driberg did make sexual lunges at other MPs (as well as a young Mick Jagger), Callaghan seems to have remained untroubled by Driberg's advances. With Driberg dead, Callaghan thought it best not to disturb a hornets' nest by complaining about Wheen's revelation.

Flash forward to *The Spectator*'s Parliamentarian of the Year lunch and Sunny Jim finds himself clutching *The Spectator*'s Elder Statesman of the Year award in one hand and the object of Driberg's admiration in the other in a lavatory at the Savoy Hotel. In the next trap is yours truly, aka William Hickey.

As he prepared himself for the job in hand, I said 'hello' and congratulated him on his honour... He beamed good-naturedly and thanked me. Then he asked, 'And what do you do?' I replied nonchalantly, 'Oh, I'm William Hickey of the *Daily Express*.' Sunny Jim's smile vanished instantly as a cloud of intense annoyance filled his face.

Without another word he turned his left shoulder to me, shielding his front, and proceeded to urinate on his shoes. I had never sought to sneak a glance at Jim's honourable member and, hand on heart, have no idea if it had retained the awesome dimensions that had so impressed Driberg.

The Savoy Hotel's most famous resident at that time was Irish actor Richard Harris. He lived there until his death in 2002. At the time he was in the midst of a late career revival as Dumbledore in the film versions of J. K. Rowling's *Harry Potter*. He would have hated the *Sun* splash headline: 'Dumbledore is Dead'. What about *This Sporting Life* and *A Man Called Horse*?

In the years before his death we had become friends and met frequently in the Coal Hole pub next door to the Savoy. After a twelve-year abstinence, Richard had resumed drinking. But there was no more hell-raising. In truth, he was lonely and adjourned to the Coal Hole in search of company and conversation – mostly about his beloved Munster rugby.

One afternoon I found myself in the Strand and, with Mother's Day approaching, popped into a branch of Clinton's and bought a card to send to my mammy in County Cavan.

Planning to write the message and enclose a modest cheque while sipping a pint in the nearby Coal Hole, I encountered Richard hunched over a pint of Boddingtons at a table just inside the door. He beckoned me over. Soon our table was laden with a profusion of empty glasses. We drank a considerable number of pints and talked mostly about our mutual friend Jimmy Waldron, known as the Muncher (more about him later). The Muncher was a subject of great amusement to the Limerick-born Harris. Eventually his eyes alighted on my Mother's Day card. 'What's that?' he asked. I explained. He nodded, sipped his Boddingtons and asked, 'How much are you sending her for Mother's Day?' 'I thought £50,' I replied. Harris erupted: 'You mean Cavan bastard, send her £100.'

He then opened the card, borrowed my ballpoint and began feverishly scribbling a message. It was a sweet bulletin wishing her well and talking me up. I then wrote an Allied Irish Bank cheque for £100 and inserted it atop

Richard's scrawled handwritten epistle, which filled the entire two sides of the Hallmark.

On the front of the card and on the accompanying pink envelope were two brown, matching rings of beer accidentally imprinted by the bottoms of our pint glasses.

A week after dispatching the card, my mother telephoned. She was delighted with the cheque, but she couldn't read a word of Harris's indecipherable handwriting. I identified the writer: 'Richard Harris!' she exclaimed. 'Isn't he lovely!' Somehow she then got it into her head that Harris had also signed the cheque. Until she succumbed to dementia, Richard was up there with the Pope and Padre Pio in my mater's pantheon of heroes.

At the conclusion of a subsequent Coal Hole session, Harris invited me to join him in his Savoy suite next door to watch his favourite team Chelsea play in a Champions League quarter final. I declined and, producing a gilt-edged invitation, explained that I was walking a few blocks to the HQ of Penguin Books for a drinks party to celebrate the publication of the millionth paperback copy of Frank McCourt's *Angela's Ashes*.

'Would you like to come?' I asked, thinking that Harris would be delighted to join the congratulatory throng surrounding his fellow Limerick-born literary success.

I was very much mistaken. 'Frank McCourt!'

exclaimed Harris. 'That wanker. I wouldn't cross the street to piss on him.' It transpired that there had been a long-running feud between the actor and the Pulitzer prize-winning writer.

To his dying day, Harris was convinced McCourt had greatly exaggerated his account of his impoverished childhood on the banks of the Shannon. Before fame swept McCourt to riches and celebrity, Harris knew him as a thirsty New York lecturer he occasionally encountered when touring the US with his lucrative earner, the musical *Camelot*.

I didn't know at the time but, prior to writing *Angela's Ashes*, Frank and his younger brother Malachy regularly performed a stand-up routine about their colourful Limerick childhood in bars and saloons in Manhattan. Their aged mother Angela frequently turned up to shout, 'Lies! Not true!' She was distressed by the destitute ornamentation of the McCourt life in Limerick.

Mischievously, Harris said, 'When you see McCourt, ask him what happened to his mother's ashes. I know he fucking lost them.'

Another sip of Boddingtons and Harris told the story:

When his mother died he hadn't two bob to rub together.

He wanted to ship her ashes to Limerick to be scattered

over the family grave. I was touring in *Camelot* and helped himself and his brother Malachy out with cash to pay for the shipping.

Frank went to a cheap shipper in Queens and he lost his mother's ashes. He fuckin' lost them. You ask him.

We finished our drinks and agreed to reconvene the following week at the Coal Hole. I meandered to the Penguin HQ and, glass of wine in hand, gravitated towards Frank McCourt. He was being lionised by the usual circling meteorites of literary female totty who looked at him with unrequited adoration.

I introduced myself. He was beaming in delight with the attention. Then, apropos of nothing, I asked, 'Tell me, Frank, what happened to your mother's ashes?' The transformation was instant and extraordinary. He grabbed me by the throat and pushed me up against the boardroom wall.

'Harris sent you!' he screamed. 'Richard Harris fucking sent you. You tell Harris I found my mother's ashes. You go and tell him that.'

Having upset the famous author, I was asked to leave the soirée. A badge of honour in my profession, I was unfazed, though my neck was a little sore. A week later, over more pints of Boddingtons in the Coal Hole, I told

Harris that McCourt had tried to strangle me. He was helpless with mirth; he couldn't stop laughing.

'He's a fucking chancer. He made up his childhood and he lost his mother's ashes. What a fraud!'

Then, in 2002, Richard died. And before Frank McCourt joined him on the banks of the celestial Shannon seven years later, I met McCourt again at an Irish embassy party in Belgravia. It was a reception for his final book *Teacher Man* (his earlier follow-up to *Angela's Ashes* entitled *'Tis* was described by one reviewer as "'Tisn't').

He recognised me and had the good grace to apologise for grabbing me by the throat when we last met as Harris's unwelcome emissary at Penguin.

He said, 'I can tell you now. Yes, we did lose our mother's ashes. Malachy and I had too much to drink in a Manhattan bar and we left them behind ... but we did eventually retrieve them.'

I first met Harris through our mutual friend Jimmy 'the Muncher' Waldron, a character straight from the imagination of Damon Runyon. Shortly after meeting the Muncher in 1986, I interviewed Richard for my Dublin newspaper – I was then London correspondent of the *Irish Press*. He was living at the time in the Halcyon, a luxury boutique hotel in Holland Park.

We got on swimmingly. He knew how to provide

good copy, particularly when, mid-interview, a hand-some, well-upholstered Polish chambermaid arrived to change the sheets. Harris was changing at the time and was without his trousers. He winked at me and started playfully chasing the girl around the king-sized bed.

During the course of the chat he disclosed that he had sent his son Jared, then a teenager, for experimen-tal treatment to a renowned drugs rehabilitation facility in the US. He asked that this disclosure remain off the record. I agreed.

To supplement my meagre stipend from Dublin, I then regularly sold stories to the Fleet Street gossip columns. I offered the nugget about Richard's son to Peter Tory on the *Daily Star*. It was duly published.

Despite the veracity of the story, Harris sued. His argument was breach of confidence and my promise not to publish. *Star* proprietor the diminutive booby Lord Stevens had recently paid out millions after losing the famous Jeffrey Archer 'Has she fragrance?' libel case. Stevens was itching for a court fight he could win. Harris seemed a perfect target.

Naively, I agreed to give evidence for the *Star* in the knowledge that any high-profile court case would alert my employers in Dublin to my extra-curricular activi-ties with London's loathed red tops.

Richard's appearance at the High Court in the Strand was one of his greatest performances. At the time, the IRA were still killing people with car bombs in London and elsewhere and Harris had previously made supportive noises about the Provos while touring America with *Camelot*.

The *Star*'s QC asked Harris about this support. Bespectacled, his long hair combed back, Harris addressed the jury from the witness box. 'You may not be aware that I have recently condemned the IRA while in the US. As a result, the Provisional IRA have placed me under sentence of death. Because of that...' (here he halted, dropped his head and choked) '...because of the IRA, I am unable to visit my aged mother in Limerick.'

As he stifled sobs, at least one of the largely female jury prised open her handbag and reached for a tissue. But game, set and match for Harris was to come the following day.

I was called to the witness box. Under oath I was a shifty and unconvincing witness. It didn't help that Richard had chosen to sit alongside his lawyer in the well of the court just below the witness box, staring intently at me.

Fingers in his waistcoat pockets, the bewigged and pompous brief for Harris looked benignly at the jury as he asked, 'Mr McEntee, how much did you get for this piece of tittle-tattle?' 'Thirty pounds,' I replied wanly.

With a nod to the jury, his hands now clutching the collars of his gown, the lawyer boomed, 'Thirty pieces of silver!'

The case was widely reported, particularly when an extract from my Irish interview was read out in court recalling his antics with the chambermaid at the Halcyon.

This also made headlines in the Irish newspapers. Éamon de Valera, owner of my employers the *Irish Press*, wondered aloud what his multitasking London correspondent was doing in the High Court giving evidence on behalf of the *Daily Star*.

The case collapsed and Harris settled out of court for £80,000. Lord Stevens demanded an inquiry. My days as London correspondent of the *Irish Press* were numbered.

An unfortunate offshoot of my legal action with Richard Harris was the strain on my friendship with Jimmy 'the Muncher' Waldron. This 25-stone man mountain was a close friend of Richard and his late brother Dermot. Born in London of parents from Leitrim, he claimed to be the purveyor of expensive marble kitchens, but I never saw him work a day in his life. His triple vocation was eating, drinking and smoking.

I first met him one Sunday afternoon tucking into a gargantuan lunch at the long communal table in the Chelsea Arts Club. He was introduced as the Muncher by Dr David MacSweeney, a bohemian Irish-born psychiatrist and former Irish international rugby player.

I was with my then wife Colette and Muncher was not only big, but talked big. His conversation was peppered with celebrity names and exotic locations. He claimed to live in a penthouse flat directly opposite the fashionable Queen's Elm pub a short stagger from the arts club.

Only when I had a chance encounter with him outside a North Wembley launderette weeks later did I discover the truth. Clutching a bundle of shirts, vests and underpants and puffing on a Rothmans, he sheepishly pointed across the road to his real residence – his late sister's council flat. His circle of friends included John Murphy Jr, the Irish building magnate, and Dermot Harris, Richard's brother and manager.

During yet another of Richard Harris's US tours with the musical *Camelot* – he owned the rights and made millions from it – Dermot dropped dead suddenly in Chicago. Harris, alias King Arthur, summoned the Muncher, his knight in shining armour, to bring his brother's body home for burial in Limerick.

Before Richard and I fell out over the *Daily Star* betrayal, Richard invited me to his suite at the Savoy Hotel. It was the early '80s and he had not yet resumed drinking. Living on a tedious diet of mostly muesli and yogurt, he was fit as a flea but bored with the monotony of his health regime. He had invited the Muncher to eat his way through the menu so he could enjoy the sumptuous grub vicariously.

I arrived at his top-floor suite overlooking the Thames to find the besuited Muncher ensconced at a small table in the middle of the sitting room. He was already working his way through a full English breakfast. Harris beckoned me to sit alongside him on the sofa as he marvelled at the Muncher.

'Isn't he fucking great?!' exclaimed Richard. 'I wish I could eat like that.'

Breakfast dispatched, a waiter arrived with another steaming platter. It was solemnly placed before the Muncher and unveiled. Roast beef! While I was there, a succession of white-jacketed waiters arrived holding shoulder-high silver salvers. In the course of the afternoon, Muncher, po-faced, dignified, worked his way through roast chicken and Dover sole as well as the roast beef. This was followed by a chocolate brownie the size of a breeze block, cheesecake, ice cream and even some trifle. All washed down with claret. It was a gluttonary triumph. By the final contented burp, Jimmy bore an alarming resemblance to Monty Python's doomed

Mr Creosote (thankfully he didn't explode). Harris's enjoyment of the spectacle was almost sexual.

Our next meeting was at Muncher's bedside in a north London clinic. Feeling unwell, he'd had a daft brainwave. He signed up with BUPA, the private medical insurance company, listed all his ailments and then immediately booked himself in to the clinic for what he called 'a complete MOT'. Harris and I went to visit and found the Muncher, unsurprisingly, eating his way through the clinic's excellent menu. 'I've even had my dandruff and my ingrown toenail done,' he boasted between mouthfuls.

BUPA subsequently baulked at the £6,000 bill. Muncher's action was similar to purchasing fire insurance after the house had been incinerated. Muncher's reaction to the massive bill was to ask his friend the psychiatrist Dr David MacSweeney to write to BUPA explaining that Jimmy was temporarily insane when he erroneously filled in the application form. Despite MacSweeney's fraudulent letter, BUPA demanded payment. At the time of his death in 1995, Muncher was paying BUPA back at the rate of £5 per week.

Harris also availed of MacSweeney's medical expertise when he fell backstage when playing Pirandello's Henry IV at the Palace Theatre Victoria. He suffered a nasty head wound requiring stitches. Fearful of insurance complications with the show, he summoned MacSweeney. 'I haven't done fucking stitches since I was a medical student,' raged the psychiatrist as he stitched up Harris.

Shortly before his admission to hospital, the Muncher did me one service, though a fee of £100 was discreetly demanded. It was in 1994 and I was working for Eve Pollard's *Sunday Express*. Eve had spotted Soho chef and restaurant owner Alastair Little on Channel 4 declaring that British diners did not complain enough about inferior food and service. Eve assigned me the task of dining at Alastair's nosherie and complaining vociferously.

A good idea? No, not if the restaurant (a) has only thirty covers and (b) serves splendid fare.

The Muncher agreed to accompany me to Little's and whinge for Europe. Before ordering, smoking vociferously, he summoned a waitress and asked, 'Is there a skip outside?' She looked baffled. So did I. 'Why do you want a skip?' she asked. Pointing at the formidable collection of smouldering cigarette butts on the table, the Muncher replied, 'I'd like somewhere to empty the ashtray.'

And so it went on. He sent the oysters back claiming one was 'off', the bread roll was stale, the wine was corked, the vegetables were cold. The procession of complaints seemed endless. When he raised his hand to summon the waitress and complain that his rare to medium sirloin was too well done, I was actually shaking. Throughout this performance, the chef/proprietor Alastair glared through the open half door of his bustling kitchen at the back of the room. From his face and demeanour, and that of his white-clad fellow cooks, it was clear that there was, to put it mildly, a tense atmosphere.

On the return of Muncher's newly, lightly grilled steak, a tall, thin lady of a certain age rose to her feet from an adjoining table. 'My name is Lady Preston,' she boomed, addressing us like a church assembly. 'I have been coming here regularly for ten years. Your behaviour is disgraceful.'

After a whispered conversation between the waitress (who turned out to be a shareholder in the bustling establishment) and Alastair over the open kitchen hatch, she marched back to the table.

I abruptly confessed my identity. It only fuelled the already raging furnace of rage. 'We would like you to leave – now,' she barked, neatly sliding the bill onto the table. I tried in vain to explain my mission, but Alastair had dashed from the kitchen. He simply declared, 'Out – NOW!' and pointed at the door. The Muncher and I spontaneously stood to attention, dropped our napkins to the table, still laden with Alastair's excellent fare, and walked out said door. In the nearby French House, where we had adjourned for a restorative bottle of Chablis, Muncher insisted the food had been inferior. It wasn't.

The following morning from my work station at the *Sunday Express*, I telephoned Mr Little at home to explain. He listened patiently and said, 'There is a play called *The Kitchen* by Arnold Wesker where a chef ruins the life of a restaurateur. Last night you ruined my life.' Ouch. In mitigation, I managed to persuade Eve not to run the piece.

Whatever the shortcomings of the Muncher's friend Richard Harris, the Limerick-born movie star was certainly a generous man and didn't baulk at lavishly tipping staff who looked after him at his £2,000-a-week permanent suite at the Savoy. No one would ever accuse his fellow Hollywood star Sean Connery of a similar weakness.

When Connery's wife Micheline bought the rights to the hit play *Art* and opened in the West End in 1996, Connery hosted the first-night party at the Mall Gallery, half a mile from Buckingham Palace.

I was working for the Londoner's Diary at the *Evening Standard* at the time and went to the opening night and the subsequent 'party'. I spotted a scowling Albert Finney, who, along with co-star Tom Courtenay, had turned up to accept the congratulations of London's moveable feast of freeloaders, of which I was an integral part.

I shook hands with Albert, who introduced me to his two sisters. They had travelled from Leeds to see their brother in Connery's production of the French play. 'Can you believe it?', shouted Finney above the babble of conversation. 'Connery has only installed a pay bar! I had to pay cash for my sisters' drinks.'

Now, free drink remains a crucial cornerstone of all first-night shindigs – beer and wine are the usual liquid staples, champagne if the backers are confident and free with their money. The Scottish-born former 007 star was in no danger of falling into the latter category.

After listening to Finney's tirade, I elbowed my way to confront Sean, who was standing near the door flanked by two po-faced hunks of raw beef in tuxedos. I introduced myself. He nodded. I leaned forward to gain access to his ear. 'Albert Finney is complaining about having to buy drinks for his sisters. Why have you installed a pay bar?'

Connery blinked and his lips formed an unmistakeable sneer. He made eye contact with one of the jumbo tuxedos standing alongside me. After a sharp nod of his head downwards, I felt firm hands under each of my oxters. Lifted ever so slightly off the ground, I was propelled backwards towards the door. Like receding daylight in a railway tunnel, Connery's face got smaller and smaller. The last thing I saw through the door as I was deposited onto the tree-lined gravel of the Mall was Connery grinning.

Connery's friend and fellow countryman the director Joe McGrath very much enjoyed my story. Shortly before the opening of *Art* he had accompanied a kilt-clad Sean to an awards ceremony in Edinburgh. He and half a dozen of Sean's chums decided to travel the mile distance to the Balmoral Hotel for late-night drinks. As they peered left and right for a taxi, Connery hopped on a bus. One of his famous nods to the driver confirmed that Sean would not be paying for the trip.

Connery and Harris were not friends, but Harris did enjoy the company of his fellow Irish actor, the Leeds-born Peter O'Toole.

Both had abandoned drink after achieving fame and doing considerable damage to their livers. And, like Harris, O'Toole had returned to fairly enthusiastic drinking before his death, aged eighty-one, in December 2013. His regular drinking companion was the brilliant character actor Ronnie Fraser.

Despite early fame in movies such as *The Flight of the Phoenix*, Ronnie was down on his luck in the early years of the new century. Decently, O'Toole agreed to take part in Chris Evans's ground-breaking *TFI Friday* show for Channel 4 on the condition that the out-of-work Ronnie be wheeled onto the weekly live gig as well. The pair had much mirth lampooning Shakespeare's *Hamlet* and generally having fun on the live show.

Ronnie and Peter frequently drank in the Haverstock Arms, close to Ronnie's Maida Vale flat. After a skinful, they would regularly meander the short distance to Ronnie's abode to roll a reefer or two and enjoy some grade-A cannabis. O'Toole delighted in telling the story of the night a well-refreshed Ronnie swayed at the closed door of the boozer and beckoned to a passing policeman... 'Constable, Constable,' spluttered Ronnie in his faux-posh accent. 'Can you help Mr O'Toole and I?' The young bobby nodded that he could. 'Do you have a sniffer dog about your person?' The policeman clearly wasn't accompanied by a sniffer dog. 'No,' he replied. Ronnie gazed at him and asked, 'Do you have a sniffer dog at your police station?' The officer said there were a number of such dogs at the local station. 'Would it be possible,' asked Ronnie, 'would it be at all possible to borrow a sniffer dog?' The bobby asked why. Straight-faced, Ronnie replied, 'Well, you see, I've mislaid my stash. I know it is in the flat somewhere. The dog would be of immense assistance finding it. Can you help?' Mercifully, the bobby ordered the inebriated thespians, by now unable to contain their mirth, to move along and go home.

I had less fun with two brilliant writers, P. D. James and Ruth Rendell. Both members of the House of Lords, Baroness James and Baroness Rendell were close friends but could never be described as hell-raisers. Good-time girls they were not. And, in my case, they confirmed the adage of not suffering fools gladly.

In 2010, I managed to persuade Baroness James, then approaching her ninetieth birthday, to take part in a feature entitled 'Me and My School Photo' (she had attended a school in Oxford, where cartoonist Ronald Searle was inspired by her and her schoolmates to create the anarchic girls of St Trinian's). She agreed on condition she could vet the copy. She returned the piece, having deleted a reference to the quaint 1930s custom of Boots the chemist providing a uniformed nurse at a special counter to dispense sanitary towels to her and her school mates.

Here is her email:

Dear John,

I'm afraid I hadn't realised that the article would be in my voice. I never normally agree to any article appearing under my name unless I have personally written it.

However, you have used most of my own words from the diary/autobiography so I don't think there will be a lot of alteration.

I would, however, like the sentences about sanitary protection in the 1930s to be deleted. These are fine in a book where they form part of a longer narrative, but in a short article this emphasis gives the impression that I am somewhat obsessed with menstruation. I am therefore deleting this part and will send you an amended copy – incorporating the typos and other grammatical alterations which Joyce has corrected in my absence – by the end of the day, or first thing tomorrow morning. I hope this is acceptable.

With kind regards

P. D. James

And then, just before the piece appeared in the *Mail*'s weekend magazine, she emailed me to ask that her fee be forwarded to her agent. I explained that I was the one getting a fee for the interview and I had forwarded the piece, not for rewriting, but as a courtesy. She replied that as former chairman of PEN she felt aggrieved that writers were not being properly recompensed but, in this particular case, she would waive her fee.

I experienced a different kind of misunderstanding with her chum Baroness Rendell of Babergh, alias Ruth Rendell. We met at a table upstairs in the Ivy restaurant to talk about her support for the Royal National Institute for the Blind. I had got the wrong end of the stick and launched a Gatling gun-like delivery of queries about deafness.

'Are you deaf?' 'No,' she answered curtly. 'Hard of hearing?' 'No,' she snapped. 'Has anyone in your family suffered from deafness?' 'No,' she bristled. 'Look, what are all these questions about deafness? I am here for the National Institute for the Blind.

Not a good start to the gentle interrogation of a woman who was eighty-three at the time. It didn't help that Baroness Rendell was also still in mourning for actor George Baker, who brought her creation Inspector Wexford to televisual life and had died just before our chat.

With twenty-four Wexford novels, fourteen Barbara Vines and dozens of other books, Ruth Rendell didn't have to listen to guff from blundering journalists. 'I've answered more questions than you'll ever ask,' was one brittle reply to a query about her much-protected private life.

She gave Agatha Christie's enduring lady detective short shrift, explaining:

I think the idea of a Miss Marple figure solving a crime

is ridiculous. I once wrote a short story where this old lady sits in her window snooping and gets it all wrong, pinning the crime on a totally innocent neighbour. That's much more likely. Agatha Christie is a menace.

I mentioned briefly my experience of working for Eve Pollard, aka Lady Lloyd, editor of the *Sunday Express*, in the early '90s. My first encounter with Eve was not fortuitous. Gleaning gossip for the *Standard*'s Londoner's Diary, I was at the 1989 Labour Party conference in Brighton when I came across Eve in the bar of the Grand Hotel.

As I reported for *The Oldie*, it was past midnight and the dimly lit room was thronged with high-spirited journalists.

It was the second night of the conference and party leader Neil Kinnock and his local Welsh male voice choir had just finished belting out songs from the Valleys in a hall behind the Grand Hotel.

Kinnock's acolyte Alastair Campbell, then political editor of the *Daily Mirror* and a yet-to-be-reformed boozer, was multitasking. Appropriately lubricated, he was playing the bagpipes and simultaneously attempting a reel.

Behind him, a glass of champagne in hand, was an equally well-refreshed Keith Waterhouse, whose jerking and knee-bending suggested he was rehearsing for

Riverdance in advance of its invention at the Eurovision song contest in Dublin five years later.

In front of the musical duo, dozing on a bar stool, was Anthony Bevins, political editor of *The Independent*. Standing at the marble-topped bar was right-wing columnist Bruce Anderson, deep in conversation with Eve, then editor of the *Sunday Mirror*.

Arriving thirsty from Kinnock's sing-song, future *Panorama* reporter John Sweeney and I edged up to the bar in search of refreshment. I spotted the statuesque Miss Pollard and, breaking away from Sweeney, attempted to introduce myself.

Bruce Anderson, dazed after more than a whiff of the cork, took exception. 'Fuck off, potato head,' he said sweetly, referring to my Hibernian roots. I didn't reply, but simply whipped off his thick-lensed spectacles and put them in my jacket pocket. Blinking owlishly, Bruce swung a wild punch in my general direction, but missed and instead struck Miss Pollard's protruding embonpoint. As she staggered back, the noise woke Anthony Bevins from his semi-slumber further along the bar.

'Anderson, you cunt,' he roared as he accelerated towards Bruce. Arching his elbow, he tried to deliver an uppercut. He missed. Poor Eve's chest was again the unfortunate recipient.

Bevins began to wrestle with the myopic Anderson. Leaping into space like a blubbery Butch Cassidy and a skinny Sundance Kid, they toppled over onto Campbell.

Domino-like, the bagpiper fell back. He had made contact with Keith Waterhouse, whose uncoordinated energetic jigging was immediately brought to a halt. The author of *Billy Liar* and *Jeffrey Bernard is Unwell* tumbled to the floor. He was followed quickly by Campbell, then Anderson, then Bevins.

The bagpipes continued to wail as the foursome rolled about the Axminster trying to disentangle themselves. I felt a hand in my jacket pocket. It was Eve Pollard. Had my romantic luck changed? Alas, no. 'Give me Bruce's glasses,' she snapped. She found them in my pocket. Sweeney suggested it was time we made a discreet exit. So we did.

Afterwards, I discovered that Bruce had at some stage written about mixed marriages. Bevins had been married to a lady from India. He had nursed a grievance until that eventful night in the Grand Hotel.

This Wild West recollection from 1989 is not to celebrate the joys of booze-fuelled brawling among members of the Fourth Estate, but it does underline the depressing reality of modern-day Fleet Street.

Bruce and I recently shared a bottle or two with Boisdale's Ranald Macdonald and Brucie insisted he had never called me 'potato head'. 'I called you a famine dodger,' he explained helpfully.

There was an unexpected postscript to the Grand Hotel incident. Two years after the late-night seaside punch-up, Pollard was the newly installed editor of the *Sunday Express*.

Unbeknownst to her, I had been hired as a feature writer by her new deputy, Craig MacKenzie. Deal done, he introduced me to Eve. As we shook hands, she peered at me with a quizzical look and asked, 'Haven't I seen you somewhere before?' I lied. 'Noooo, Eve.'

I could fill half an acre of *Who's Who* with all the jobs I was appointed to by Eve, including royal correspondent, editor of the London section, arts editor and feature writer. Eve's stewardship of the *Sunday Express* was often bizarre, squeezed as it was like one of Eve's too-small designer dresses between her commitments to *Through the Keyhole* and other lucrative TV jobs.

She treated the old guard, lingering from the days of editor Sir John Junor, like something she had trodden on in the street. Literary editor Graham Lord was ordered to report for duty on Saturdays, where he sat in magnificent isolation on the fourth floor reading forthcoming books. The last straw was when Eve asked him to join a group of reporters telephoning top London hotels on a Saturday afternoon enquiring about the possibility of hiring a room by the hour. Eve had heard that even the finest establishments in London were 'hot-sheet' hotels where couples could adjourn for afternoon trysts.

Eve had also taken control of Graham's weekly charity book sale, the proceeds of which went to nearby St Bart's Hospital. After her arrival, the money raised by staff buying hardbacks for £1 and paperbacks for 50p was reallocated to a special fund to finance champagne-guzzling sessions for staff to celebrate circulation rises.

There weren't many of those. Indeed, this wasn't the first time I'd been witness to Eve's rather flippant attitude to spending other people's money. I was editor of the London section at the time, and one Saturday my secretary was seconded to travel with Eve's long-suffering chauffeur Ray to Bond Street to buy a list of cosmetics itemised in a list provided by Eve. The girl sought my advice, saying Eve had given her £40 in cash but the list of items would surely cost more than that. I suggested she ask Ray, who had long experience of Lady Lloyd's peccadillos.

The cosmetics cost in excess of £100 and, returning to the newsroom, Ray, who had charged the cost of the unguents, anti-ageing creams, perfumes and lipstick to his credit card, sought reimbursement from Eve. Trying to edit the following day's *Sunday Express* on a bustling newsroom floor, Eve directed Ray to her fourth-floor office, where a secretary would eventually reimburse him.

Squirrel-like *Sunday Express* gardening editor Max Davidson had been demoted to six-day-a-week subbing duties. But his spring, summer and autumn Sundays were spent touring the country at gardening roadshows, doling out advice and free copies of the paper to green-fingered readers.

When Pollard's deputy, the world-class booby Charles Golding, noticed that Max's expenses included the cost of a double room in the hotels he was obliged to stay in from Holyhead to York, he was called in for a grilling.

He explained to the bow-tied wonder that, as he worked six days a week, he hardly saw his wife. Thus, she accompanied him on the gardening roadshow activities. Hence the double room. But, in mitigation, he explained to Max that he didn't claim an evening meal, taking the precaution of bringing a cool box with some sandwiches and a Thermos flask of tea for hotel-room tête-a-têtes with his beloved.

Golding decreed that in future he could charge for the room only if his wife helped with the gardening road-shows. So Mrs Davidson agreed to don a Rupert the

Bear costume (the *Express* owned Rupert) and prance about the roadshows as her husband Max pontificated on Japanese ragwort and ailing fuchsias.

While Eve could be nasty, her deputy Golding was malevolent. Baby-faced, bespectacled, with a shock of dark hair and a white shirt fronted with a bright bow tie, his fundamental talents were lying and back-stabbing.

Ostensibly devoted to Eve, he was fundamentally disloyal, as manifested in his behaviour when I asked Eve if I could attend a *Private Eye* lunch at the Coach and Horses in Soho.

At the time, the *Eye* was running a series of well-informed stories about the behaviour of *Express* proprietor Lord Stevens and Lord and Lady Lloyd at the *Daily* and *Sunday Express* in the magazine's Street of Shame section.

Steven's obsession with *Private Eye* eventually led him to install an alert on the *Express* switchboard. If any employee made a telephone call or sent a fax to the *Eye* (it was just before the widespread use of the internet) the switchboard lit up with the offending extension.

Editor Ian Hislop had been sending me invitations to the regular fortnightly lunches for some time. I had been declining, making a series of feeble excuses. After the arrival of another invite, I received a back-up call from Hislop's flunkey Christopher Silvester, stating that if I didn't turn up, the next edition of the *Eye* would publish an item saying that Pollard had banned me.

I decided to bring the invite to Eve.

'Should I attend?' I asked. Effusively, she replied, 'Of course you must go. Please give Ian my love.'

As I emerged from her office, Golding was outside the door, clearly eavesdropping. He beckoned me into his adjoining cubicle. 'You are going to the *Eye* lunch,' he stated. 'When you see Hislop, will you tell him that *I* really edit the paper. Eve is never here. She is always off filming *Through the Keyhole* or working for the BBC.'

Cravenly, I tipped the side of my nose and felt like Eric Idle in the Monty Python 'nudge-nudge, say no more' sketch. But Golding wasn't finished. Stung by the *Eye*'s description of him as Charles 'Interesting' Golding, he added, 'Will you tell them I'd like to be called Charles "I'm in Charge" Golding.' I went to the lunch and there was no mention of Eve, let alone Golding, over the melon and steak.

But Golding did make the Street of Shame in 1995, when I finally escaped from Eve's clutches to work for her husband Nick on the *Daily Express* a floor below. I had organised a farewell drinks party at Doggett's, the pub on the other side of Blackfriars Road, adjacent to the Thames. I had invited most of my colleagues and, on the day of the shindig, put my head around the door of Golding's office to say, 'Charles, I know everyone else thinks you are a cunt, but I'd like to invite you to my party.' I left him spluttering and demanding names of his detractors.

His third-floor office had a splendid view of Blackfriars Bridge, and he had equipped himself with a pair of high-powered binoculars. During a meeting with Golding, feature writer James Steen pointed at the binoculars on his desk and asked him what they were for. Sitting with his back to the bridge, Golding boasted that he often spotted newsworthy dramas on the bridge or the river – drownings, crashes and such like – which made stories for the paper.

As Golding spouted, Steen could see over his shoulder a group of armed police in the middle of Blackfriars Bridge surrounding a man lying on the roadway after being ordered out of a car that was boxed in by three police vehicles.

Golding was blissfully unaware of the excitement.

The real purpose of the binoculars was for Golding to spy on his rival, Alan Cochrane, the head of news who had been poached from the *Mail on Sunday*. A brilliant journalist, he was a Scot who liked a drink and regularly refreshed himself at lunchtime in El Vino's on the other side of the bridge (not the Fleet Street mothership but what we called 'El Vino Sur Mer').

Alan often lunched late and was invariably making his way back to HQ at 4 p.m., with Golding's binoculars monitoring his progress. Pollard was kept well-informed of Alan's drinking habits. He was often accompanied by City editor Dominic Prince, a roly-poly figure once described by Michael Toner as 'waddling about the newsroom with the hint of a permanent erection'.

Prince too enjoyed daily refreshment at El Vino's. But when he finished his smoked salmon, champagne (daily half-bottle) and house claret (one bottle) and left with Cochrane, he usually summoned a taxi to ferry him the short distance across the bridge to Ludgate House. Alan put it down to indolence, but canny Prince knew about the binoculars.

Prince was, along with William Sitwell and India Knight, that rare breed of journalist on the good ship Pollard. They liked a laugh.

Sitwell, who later landed a job as feature writer on the *Daily Mail* on the back of his friendship with the still missing Lord Lucan's son George, has blossomed as a telly chef and editor of *Waitrose Food*.

His great scoop was developing a friendship with Pippa Middleton, sister of Kate, who married Prince William, a candidate for the *Guinness World Records* accolade as the dullest royal of the twenty-first century.

Pippa enthralled Sitwell's readers with her recipe for ice. No, it's not a misprint: 'tis ice.

William Sitwell is a charming cove, as evidenced by our alcohol-fuelled lunch at the fashionable Oxo Tower, adjacent to the *Sunday Express* office on Blackfriars Road.

Mid-munch we were interrupted by a passing friend of mine, 'Mad' Frankie Fraser, a gangster from the Kray twins' era who, having spent most of his adult life in prison, was now a celebrity of sorts. Frankie's main claim to fame was his dexterity with pliers, removing unwillingly the teeth of fellow villains.

Wearing an overcoat and his trademark demented look, Frankie had stopped at our table to say hello. I said to William, 'Have you met my friend Mad Frankie Fraser?' William patted his lips with his napkin, offered his hand and said, 'May I call you Mr Mad?' Frankie's eyes darkened and his brow furrowed in a quizzical look I did not discern as welcoming.

Quick as a flash, he had extracted from his overcoat a jumbo-size set of pliers – the sort that B&Q sell to extract bolts from bulldozers – and pointed them at Sitwell. One of his shoes was resting on my lap as he threatened Sitwell with the bolt cutters. 'Is he taking the piss?' he asked me sweetly as William's molar hovered into view.

To his credit, William eyed Frankie, laughed and went back to his risotto. The spell was broken. Mad Frankie slipped his tool back into the pocket of his overcoat and was gone.

For me it was a rare jolly moment in a miserable regime. Eve's principal focus as editor of the *Sunday Express* was on her ambitions to be a TV star. She was a regular on David Frost's *Through the Keyhole* and on the BBC's annual coverage of Ascot. But she wanted more.

Her chum Greg Dyke had saved TV-am from closure with the introduction of a puppet called Roland Rat. Eve was one of the team he introduced at the rejuvenated breakfast TV station. She still wallowed in the glory of her time at TV-am. In the egg-cup-adorned studios in Camden, Golding was a lowly fetch-and-carry merchant who barnacled himself to Pollard and waited for his career to soar. Tragically, it did.

I was Eve's media correspondent when Dyke was asked to perform a similar miracle with ailing GMTV. On the Saturday morning – the day after he had announced his plans at a press conference – Eve asked me to call Greg at home and quiz him about his resurrection of TV-am.

Dyke knew immediately what I was after. 'I get it,' he told me after complaining about the intrusion into his precious weekend time with his children. 'Eve wants me to say she was part of the TV-am team so she can put her name in her own paper. Well, she was part of the revival of TV-am.'

As I was scribbling Greg's answers, I noticed the bow-tied wonder gesticulating at the end of my desk. Golding was pointing at himself and mouthing, 'Ask him about me!'

As Greg's ramblings finished I said, 'Oh, and what about Charles Golding? Did he have a part to play?' Greg asked, 'Who?' I repeated Golding's name as the nincompoop nodded frantically in front of me. 'Oh, Golding. Yes, I remember that idiot now. I'd completely forgotten about him.'

When I hung up, Golding panted, 'What did he say about me?'

I replied sweetly, 'He said you were an idiot.'

Bafflingly, Eve promoted Golding from features editor, where he was useless, to deputy editor, where he was inept. When he introduced himself at his first meeting as features editor he boasted of writing a definitive book about rats, adding, 'Did you know that in London you are never more than twelve feet away from a rat?' The assembled writers, including myself, Graham Lord, Scarth Flett, Sally Staples and Jay Iliff, gazed intently and in unison at King Rat.

While Golding was pure evil and Eve unpleasant, she could also be plain daft.

Once she spotted a two-page advertisement in the *Financial Times* announcing a new British Airways red-eye service out of New York's JFK to London Heathrow. An enticing picture showed a duvet and pillow-laden seat pushed back to make a bed. A steaming mug of cocoa completed the picture and highlighted the advantages of a blissful sleep across the Atlantic.

Somehow, Eve convinced herself that BA had introduced real beds in first class on board their Boeing 747s. Her desk was strewn with monochrome photographs of stewards serving breakfast to bunk-bedded passengers on board the old flying boats of the '30s. News editor Phil Hall was unable to convince her that they were merely conventional seats temporarily converted to beds.

It was a Wednesday and I was told to fly to New York with a photographer and return on the new service in time for Sunday's paper. 'The only way we can do that on time is to fly Concorde to New York,' I explained to Phil in the hope of dissuading Eve. 'Go ahead,' she ordered.

So, on Friday morning, Tony the photographer and I boarded the morning flight to JFK on Concorde. Cost? £5,000 each.

There were only fifteen other passengers, who looked

disdainfully on our schoolboy enthusiasm for the vintage champagne – in glasses, not little bottles – of which we greedily availed ourselves, summoning the steward by constant ding-dongs on the overhead button. Then we asked to visit the cockpit and thrilled at the slight lurch on reaching the speed of sound.

Landing at JFK, I fell foul of the dreaded US immigration when I showed them my Irish passport – at the time, thousands of my fellow countrymen and women were emigrating and staying illegally in the US. 'How long are you staying in New York, sir?' asked the Stalinist man in uniform. 'Oh, I'm going back this evening,' I explained brightly.

'Wise guy,' snapped the immigration goon, summoning a fellow officer with a wave of his hand. 'Strip-search him.' For the crime of being the only Paddy to go to the Big Apple for the day, I had a Marigold glove shoved up my rectum. I was limping slightly when I rejoined Tony the photographer in the arrivals hall.

Tony suggested buying a teddy bear at Macy's department store so I could be photographed on the return journey in my complimentary Reebok pyjamas enjoying my BA cocoa prior to a good slumber in Eve's 'bed'.

The following morning in the newsroom when Eve saw

the photos she pointed at the bear nestling next to my head. 'Where did you get that?' she snapped. I explained I'd bought it in Macy's. 'I have a receipt,' I offered, weakly. She stuck out her ample chest and barked, 'Why didn't you bring Rupert?' Strike one. The *Express* owned Rupert the Bear.

Then, peering at the photos, she shrieked, 'These aren't real beds! When Nick and I fly to Barbados, Lord King (then boss of BA) provides duvets and pillows for Nick and I. What is the difference here?' I replied, 'Cocoa.' Strike two.

With a gasp, Eve retorted, 'How much did this jolly cost?'

I replied sheepishly, 'About £10,000, Eve.' Strike three.

Apart from the strip-search, it was a grand day out. Eve and her husband Nicholas constantly sprinkled rose petals in the path of British Airways boss Lord King. In return, they enjoyed frequent free flights with BA from London to the holiday island of Barbados.

Their enthusiasm for accepting John King's hospitality is directly responsible for one of the longest-running recurring jokes in *Private Eye*: the photograph of former *Sunday Times* editor Andrew Neil in his vest and baseball cap standing alongside an unnamed dusky beauty.

The snap has been appearing on the letters page of the

Eye since 1995, mischievously encouraged by dubious readers requesting photographic evidence of middle-aged men accompanied by younger beauties.

In the twenty years that *Eye* editor Ian Hislop has gleefully succumbed to the so-called readers' requests and published yet again poor Andrew's unfortunate encounter with a young lady in a swimsuit, the former *Sunday Times* editor must have shaken his head and wondered, why, oh why?

Officially Andrew, nicknamed Brillo by the *Eye* for his fascinating hair, must regret ever posing for the so-called Photo Opportunity, with a woman frequently mistaken for his former squeeze Pamella Bordes. It isn't Bordes who was subsequently wrongly accused of taking a pair of scissors to the crotches of debonair Andrew's bespoke suits after he told her to leave his Chelsea flat.

There have been many stories about the origin of the notorious snap. I can now relate the true tale of how it came about.

In 1995, I was deputy to the much-missed Ross Benson, whose handsome visage graced his page in Sir Nicholas Lloyd's *Daily Express*. Ross, a far superior foreign correspondent than a gossip columnist, enjoyed a high-profile rivalry with the *Mail*'s Nigel Dempster.

The legendary Peter McKay nicknamed them the

Pompadoured Poltroon (Ross) and the Tonsured Seducer (Nigel) and their respective columns frequently contained jibes against each other.

Ross was on holiday one particular summer Sunday when I got a call from the editor Nick Lloyd. He was at Heathrow airport with his wife Eve. They had returned from what the newspaper industry refers to as a freebie on Barbados. They had stayed at the luxurious Sandy Lane Hotel after availing themselves of free British Airways flights provided by their friend Lord King.

While on holiday, Nick had borrowed celebrity photographer Terry O'Neill's camera and taken the image of Andrew with his Asian companion.

It was the pre-digital age and Nick had arrived at Heathrow with a roll of 35mm film containing the famous photograph. He called the Diary. I answered. He instructed me to send a motorbike to his home in Belsize Park to collect the film. It was to be processed at the *Express*. The shot of Andrew and his attractive companion was to be used that night in the Ross Benson Diary. The accompanying story? There was none.

Nick stressed that the picture was to be captioned with a 'plug' for the Sandy Lane Hotel and for British Airways.

The picture duly appeared with the required mentions. But it was not forgotten.

Soon after it began appearing in the *Eye* in response to spurious requests from 'readers'. It has been the same ever since. On the photograph's initial printing, it was suggested that Andrew found it embarrassing. Maybe that is why Hislop persists in printing it.

Neil has since described it as an example of 'public school racism' on the part of the magazine's editorial staff. But now, entwined with a delightful new, younger wife and enjoying a stellar career on television, I don't really think he cares any more.

A few weeks after my day trip to Manhattan, Eve invited some staff to join Richard Attenborough and herself at a small Soho cinema for a preview screening of Lord Dickie's excellent movie version of C. S. Lewis's *Shadowlands*. I was lucky enough to sit next to Dear Dickie in the subterranean Soho viewing room.

Lord Attenborough was, to put it mildly, prone to tears. Plonk the old boy on a podium to introduce someone or accept an award and those in the front pews were in danger of serious waterlogging. As I watched Anthony Hopkins, as Lewis, say farewell to his dying American wife, played by Debra Winger, tears cascaded down Dear Dickie's cheeks. By my calculation, he would have seen the finished film at least a dozen times beforehand. His explanation? 'Every tear a dollar, darling.'

As Eve and I and other members of staff congratulated Dickie on his tear-jerking movie, Eve asked Attenborough where C. S. Lewis's stepson lived now. Dickie explained that the boy, now a man, was extremely rich from the Lewis royalties and lived in a remote part of Ireland running a strict Christian sect. Attenborough wasn't sure of the exact location.

Without blinking, Eve turned to me and said, 'Find him for Sunday, John.'

It was then late on Thursday night. I was obliged to fly to Ireland, somehow find the grown codger, interview him and file copy by Saturday tea time... No space here to explain how, but I did it.

Suffice to say that I was obliged to spend the night with the sect, a bedroom chair lodged firmly under the doorknob. My detective work never even made the paper.

Then, just after Christmas, head of news Alan Cochrane asked me, 'What are you doing for New Year's Eve?' Assuming a party invitation was looming, I said, 'Nothing.'

'Good,' he replied. 'You can follow Virginia Bottomley around all the hospitals in Guildford.'

John Major's Health Secretary had decided to forgo her New Year's celebrations (and mine) by, Florence Nightingale-like, surprising patients at the hospitals in her constituency.

I still remember trotting down the long, dimly lit corridors of the Royal Surrey Hospital with a photographer and a Department of Health handler trailing Virginia as she glided along, striking terror into nurses and doctors trying desperately to hide alcohol earmarked for New Year's toasts less than an hour after the visit of the Secretary of State for Health.

No patients had been asked if they'd mind being photographed with the stylish minister. She was unamused when I tried to ask one particularly ill gentlemen if he wanted to be snapped with Virginia. He didn't. But, nonetheless, she posed blissfully by bedsides and shook hands with dying cancer patients and comatose occupants of NHS beds.

By 2 a.m., Virginia – charming, polite, but without a shred of self-awareness – still hadn't run out of steam, cantering off down the darkened floor of the women's floor.

She followed one shard of light from an open door and darted into a private room.

The photographer, the handler and I caught our breaths outside. Virginia emerged and beckoned to me. 'John, come in. I've found one of my constituents.'

I followed her into the room. A family of six adults was clustered around the bed. Two of them were dabbing their eyes as they wept. On the bed was the propped-up figure of an elderly lady. Connected to a drip and breathing through an oxygen mask, she was clearly about to expire. Virginia held her hand and babbled to her nearest and dearest about hospital trusts. I ran from the room and grabbed her handler. 'There is a woman about to die in there. She is surrounded by her family. They are too stunned to do anything. Go in and bring the minister out.'

A look of panic creased his face. 'I can't,' he said. 'You do it.' I had to.

We finally berthed in the ground-floor accident and emergency department. It contained all the misery of bodies broken by too much drink and drugs and fighting in the first hours of the New Year. There were two bleeding drunks lying, moaning on the floor (the harassed staff had run out of beds). A female doctor in a blood-spattered white coat administered stitches to the bloody scalp of a middle-aged man sitting on a chair. A nurse was extracting glass from the neck of a teenage girl, her mascara staining her wan face.

As an ambulance crew delivered another New Year's Eve reveller on a wheeled stretcher to this vision of NHS hell, Mrs Bottomley, handbag in hand, gingerly stepped over one of the prone drunks and proffered her hand to a distracted sister in blue. 'Hello, I'm Virginia

Bottomley. I'm the Health Secretary.' The nurse glared at Mrs Bottomley's hand and then looked straight into her face. 'I know who you are,' she snapped. 'Would you kindly fuck off?'

Mercifully, she did, allowing me to get home before first light. When I complained about the assignment to deputy editor Craig MacKenzie the following day, he explained that Virginia was a friend of Eve's and we were doing her a favour covering her hospital visits. He beckoned me to place my shoes directly against the tips of his footwear. He then leaned into my face, sniffed theatrically and declared, 'I smell burning martyr.' Oh, what japes!

To promote the *Sunday Express*, Eve had organised a deal with LBC, the London radio station – now national – for her journalists to appear on Chris Mann's live Saturday night show to review the following day's newspapers.

For some reason known only to herself, she chose one Irishman (me) and three Scotsmen (head of news Alan Cochrane, gardening editor Max Davidson and political columnist Bruce Arnold) to rotate the chore. It was a pain. We had to linger in the office until 10 p.m. on Saturday awaiting the car to ferry us to LBC HQ, then in Brook Green. Cochrane, Arnold and myself contrived to see who could appear the most sozzled on the show. It was an easy task as the *Express* building on Blackfriars Bridge was then furnished with a well-stocked bar on the ground floor called Poppins.

Presenter Chris Mann became more and more irritated by Eve's trio of increasingly well-refreshed pundits swaying their way to the microphone. Eventually, he exclaimed, 'That's it! No more.' Bruce had triumphed.

In mid-spout he had fallen to the floor followed by a cascade of early editions. Mann, his engineer and a researcher, managed to right the Scotch-filled upturned galleon during a commercial break. It was the end of the slot.

Moved from features to edit the London section – a sort of *Time Out* provided free in the London editions of the *Sunday Express* – I received a call from an irate Eve on the first weekend in my new role. She was furious over the cinema listings. She and husband Nick wanted to see the movie *Much Ado About Nothing* in their local Odeon at Swiss Cottage but my London section didn't give the times of the movie screenings. I explained that we included only the starting times of films in the West End, as to add times for every cinema from Cockfosters to Sevenoaks would take up the entire edition. Her answer?

'I want you to take out all the shit about antiques and restaurants and put in the times of every movie in every cinema in London and have it on my desk on Tuesday.'

Forlornly I trudged into work on Monday and consulted John the wizard designer and sub-editor.

There was no way we could accommodate Eve. Then he had a brainwave. 'Why don't we move Swiss Cottage into the West End?' Genius!

On Tuesday I was able to show Eve a redesigned cinema section with an enlarged box for the West End that read, alphabetically, Leicester Square, Queensway, Swiss Centre, Swiss Cottage, followed by Tottenham Court Road. For the duration of Eve's editorship, Swiss Cottage was part of the West End.

One of my innovations was a weekly diary in which a celebrity recounted his or her activities in the preceding week. Sir Trevor McDonald promised a diary that failed to materialise. I left a nagging message on his answerphone. Returning well refreshed from lunch, my secretary said, 'I've got Trevor McDonald on the phone for you.' Taking the receiver, I used a phrase familiar to my infant children when they misbehaved. 'Trevor, you little monkey. Where's the copy?' I heard a sharp intake of breath. 'What did you call me? Did you call me a monkey?' The West Indian-born doyen of newscasters was furious. 'Trevor, it was a term of endearment,' I pleaded. 'Endearment? Calling me a monkey?'

I looked around the London section desk. Two of the female reporters had their heads in their hands. The sub had his fist in his mouth. They were witnessing a car crash. It took all my skills of Irish blarney to placate Sir Trevor. Mercifully, he still takes my calls.

Unlike every other contributor, including Sir Terry Wogan, Eamonn Holmes and Lord Hailsham, Sir Trev asked for a fee. It was only £200. I gave each celebrity the option of nominating a favourite charity to receive the modest sum with the promise of an italic at the end of the piece saying: 'Sir Terry Wogan has donated his fee for this article to Children in Need.' Sir Trevor's response: 'Can I keep the fee? And you won't put an italic at the bottom saying I've kept the money?'

When Eve's new political editor Charles Lewington arrived at the *Sunday Express*, political columnist Tom Utley was ordered to vacate his desk for him.

Under protest, Tom gathered his contacts book, expense dockets and cigarettes and moved across the newsroom. Weeks later, at the Brighton party political conference of John Major's Tories, he was entering the Grand Hotel when Education Secretary John Patten spotted him and bellowed across the foyer, 'Tom, the entire Cabinet is with you!' Baffled, Tom cocked a hand to his ear and asked, 'What?' Patten boomed, 'The desk!'

As royal correspondent, I was summoned to Eve's office where head of news Alan Cochrane handed me a cheque for £10,000. 'What's that for?' I asked. Eve explained that, as Diana's confidante, Andrew Morton had just published the paperback version of his sensational book on the Princess of Wales. I was to give him the cheque in return for an interview in which he would spill more and fresh beans on the troubled princess for the *Sunday Express*. Cochrane threw his eyes theatrically to heaven.

At his Drummond Street cubbyhole, Morton eyed the cheque, pocketed it and then started to thumb through a copy of the book I could have purchased at the WH Smith emporium in nearby King's Cross station.

I listened to two hours of royal drivel, returned to the office and transcribed it for Eve. Clutching the toilet-roll length of copy, she emerged from her lair. 'This is shit, just shit. Nothing new. Offer Andrew more money.' Cochrane advised against it so it was agreed that I would tell Morton his meanderings were 'shit'. As it was Friday evening, he needed to come up with something new and worthy of ten grand. I called him. His response? 'I'll call Diana's friends tonight. Give me a ring at 7 a.m.'

I did. He replied weakly, 'Diana's friends were not in.' It was with a heavy heart that I drove to the *Express* building on Blackfriars Bridge.

Before facing the wrath of Pollard, assistant editor Jim Anderson, a towering, bald, taciturn man with a good brain, approached clutching my copy. He had underlined some of Morton's remarks where he had said that after the births of William and Harry, Diana had desperately wanted to save her marriage to Charles by getting pregnant again and having a girl.

Eureka! I was able to ghost-write Morton's by-lined nonsense for the following day's front-page splash. The headline? 'Diana: The Daughter I Can Never Have'. So effective was this fantasy that later editions of our rival the *Mail on Sunday* carried an almost identical headline under the by-line of star gossip columnist Nigel Dempster.

Nigel and I were professional friends before we went head to head against each other on rival newspapers, I as William Hickey and he with his famous column in the *Daily Mail*. Because the original William Hickey was an eighteenth-century character who had a man-servant called Munnoo, an inamorata called Charlotte and a dog called Caesar, I populated the column with characters from Hickey's eighteenth-century household. Hickey himself was an old fuddy-duddy who relied on

Munnoo and others to keep him abreast of modern life, club openings, new bands and transient figures on the gossip circuit.

I invented a fictitious character called Nigel, the oily under butler who appeared in stories in the *Express*. The real Nigel never took offence. We lunched regularly, mostly at the River Room at the Savoy. On one occasion, Nigel had booked the table for 1 p.m. I arrived from nearby Blackfriars at ten past and Nigel offered me a drink from the chilled Chablis in the ice bucket at his elbow. The waiter lifted the bottle and declared, 'Meeester Dempstur, de bottle, eet is empty.'

We had another two. Our friendship hit the buffers three years later when I had my own by-lined column in the *Express*. Nigel devoted a quarter page in the *Mail* to the death of his pet dog Tulip. The story included a photograph of the chihuahua and the prose dripped with pathos. 'The Dempster household is in mourning ... Christmas will never be the same again.'

On reading this, Chris Williams, then No. 3 on the *Express* (later to be editor), suggested I take a pot shot at Nigel following his over-the-top eulogy for Tulip. The following morning, I carried a small paragraph that read: 'The Diary is in mourning. Nigel my pet ferret has passed away after twenty-five years of faithful service. I shall miss his little nose sticking out of the bars of his bespoke cage. We shall not see his like again.' At about 11 a.m., the diary secretary Catherine took a call and, cupping her hand over the receiver, said that Nigel Dempster wanted to speak to me.

Assuming that Nigel wanted to mock my piece as very droll, I took the call. I was not prepared for the verbal onslaught. 'You Irish cunt!' he screamed. 'You Irish turd!' As I tried to get a word in edgeways, Nigel told me he was writing letters of complaint to my editor Rosie Boycott and Lord Hollick, proprietor of the *Express*.

'My dog isn't even buried yet,' he added, with a voice that suggested he was on the verge of tears. 'And I'm reporting you to the RSPCA for keeping a wild animal indoors. I shall never speak to you again.'

He then hung up. He did indeed write letters of complaint and did cut me at events. I was sad that this had occurred but thought Nigel had overreacted. Curiously, the *Express* was inundated with letters, telephone calls and emails expressing sympathy on the death of my pet ferret Nigel. So it wasn't just the world's greatest gossip columnist who believed I actually did have a ferret!

Some years later, as I was about to join the *Mail*, Nigel and I had an opportunity to be friends again. We were both invited to one of Richard Shepherd's splendid luncheons at his flagship restaurant Langan's in Stratton Place, off Piccadilly. Other guests included the great sports writer Ian Wooldridge, raconteur Ned Sherrin and the up-and-coming Sam Leith from the *Telegraph*. Nigel arrived late and spotted me at the table. 'What the fuck are you doing here?' he snapped. 'I was invited,' I replied. Nigel then flexed his cuffs, exposing a chunky gold cufflink of a rampant dog. Pointing to it, Nigel said, 'That's the dog you killed.' It was indeed a gold memorial to Tulip. I protested: 'I didn't kill your dog. I mocked its death and for that I am sorry. I underestimated how upset you would be. Will you accept my apology?' He did. We shook hands and the subject was never mentioned again.

At that stage, Nigel was in the early stages of PSP (progressive supranuclear palsy), the awful disease that had killed Dudley Moore, and would do the same to Nigel.

His initial falling over on the golf course was put down to his alcohol intake. But it became worse. In desperation, he converted to Roman Catholicism and made a pilgrimage to Lourdes, the Marian shrine in France, accompanied by his secretary Bridget, now a successful, rampantly feminist (and unfunny) stand-up comedian. Nigel wasn't cured.

Five years after his death, I was in the saloon bar of the Wellington pub in Fulham when a young man in a paint-spattered T-shirt and jeans approached my stool as I savoured the creaminess atop my perfectly poured pint of Guinness.

'Are you a journalist?' he asked speculatively. 'Yes,' I replied. 'Do you know Nigel Dempster?' he asked. Of course I knew the doyen of gossip columnists. 'Why do you ask?' I enquired of my new young acquaintance. 'Because', he replied, 'Dempster ran over me in his car while he was drunk.' It was only then I noticed the slight limp as Dempster's young victim returned to his seat in the saloon bar.

I wanted to know more. His name was Kylie Proctor, then aged twenty-six, a painter and decorator whose right leg still retained the metal supports inserted after Dempster's red Honda Accord ran over him a short distance from the Wellington. He was crossing the road with his older sister. He was never to play football again. He will always have a degree of pain but he bears no malice towards Nigel, who he was not aware had died.

It was October 1997; Kylie was aged eleven and Dempster was taking a shortcut towards Hammersmith when he collided with the schoolboy. Nigel had a reckless disregard for drink-driving rules. As his obituary in the *Daily Telegraph* in July 2007 remarked, 'Nigel disliked champagne but had a camel's thirst for Chablis.'

This led to repeated encounters with police breath-alysers. Once asked to bare his skin for a police doctor's needle in order to yield a blood sample, Dempster responded by removing his socks and instructing the physician to sink his syringe into his big toe. Another time he insisted that he had a mortal fear of needles – a phobia less apparent when he had to receive inocula-tions for a visit to Princess Margaret's holiday villa on Mustique in the West Indies.

After colliding with young Proctor, Nigel clambered out of his car and asked his prone victim if he was all right. The badly injured schoolboy clearly wasn't.

Dempster hopped back into his car and drove off at speed – but not before Kylie's sister landed a direct hit on the front wing of his Honda with a coke bottle. She also managed to get the number of Dempster's car. Nigel subsequently did use his mobile to call an ambulance.

Later that evening, he was stopped for speeding through Hammersmith. He claimed he was taking his sick Pekingese dog Posy for emergency late-night treatment. His breath smelt of alcohol. He made three attempts to provide a breath specimen at the side of the road, but each time the machine aborted the test. 'He wasn't breathing with enough force for the machine to register,' PC Stephen Billington said.

Dempster was arrested and taken to Hammersmith police station, where he later managed to provide a breath specimen with a reading of forty-five micrograms per 100 millilitres of blood. This meant he had to take a further test by giving a blood or urine sample.

When he appeared in Hammersmith Magistrates Court in February 1998 charged with drink-driving, he claimed that he had told a police doctor that he suffered from blood-injury syndrome and offered to give a urine sample. But police insisted on a blood test unless Mr Dempster could prove that he had a valid medical reason for not giving blood.

Grant Winstock, a GP and forensic medical examiner who was called to the police station to examine Mr Dempster, said that he could find no evidence that he was suffering from the blood-injury disorder.

Robin Faley, for the defence, said that Mr Dempster's phobia was so severe that he had never had a tetanus injection and took gas and valium during visits to his dentist for extensive drilling. Dr Winstock, who examined Mr Dempster for forty-five minutes, admitted that the diarist had informed him of his fear and had said that he never had injections, even when travelling to Africa and the Middle East.

'He told me he'd had a fear of needles all his life,'

Dr Winstock said. 'He said it stemmed from the age of twelve or fourteen, when some blood was taken from him. He said he tried to avoid films which showed blood.'

Dr Winstock admitted that the only way to establish whether a person was suffering from a phobia was by conducting tests under laboratory conditions. He acknowledged that he was unable to do this in a police station.

Mr Dempster told the doctor that he had not had an alcoholic drink during the previous twenty-four hours. While trying to work out what could have led to the alcohol reading on the breathalyser, Mr Dempster told the doctor that he was taking a cough medicine for asthma and bronchitis. His most recent meal before his arrest had included pears in a red wine sauce from Marks & Spencer. (This led to much ribaldry in the *Daily Mail* office about Nigel getting drunk on pears in red wine sauce.)

Nigel also attributed the smell of alcohol on his breath when stopped to concentrated garlic. The case was adjourned until the following April when Nigel added a new detail. He had drunk two pints of orange juice – unaware it had been spiked with vodka during a party the night before at his wife Lady Camilla's house.

He was convicted, banned from driving for a year, suspended pending appeal and fined £250. Leaving court, Nigel declared, 'Never complain, never explain.'

This was little consolation to the Proctor family. Kylie had spent over a month in hospital with multiple fractures. His late father was furious that Dempster had not been interviewed about the collision with his son after his arrest. Says Kylie: 'It took them eighteen weeks to talk to him about it. He was never charged. Insult was added to injury when Dempster had his drink-driving conviction quashed on appeal after claiming that a lifelong fear of needles made it impossible for him to give a blood sample.'

But, in February 2001, Nigel was at it again. This time he was charged with drink-driving after crashing into a lamp post and overturning his car. He had smashed his new green Honda into a central reservation, spun across a zebra crossing and then hit a number of bollards before rolling the car. It was just around the corner from his home on Ham Common.

It was two years before the case came before Richmond court, where it emerged that Dempster had freed himself from the wreckage and staggered straight into an off-licence.

PC Russell Yardley, who found him there, told the court:

> I saw a green Honda Accord lying on its roof. There
> was no one in the car and someone told me the driver

had gone into Wine Rack. I saw a white man with grey hair dressed in a grey suit standing at the counter. I said, 'Have you had anything alcoholic to drink?' He said, 'No, nothing.' His speech was incoherent and his eyes were glazed. I could smell liquor on his breath despite being a distance of at least three feet away.

Tests later revealed Dempster had almost double the legal alcohol limit in his bloodstream, magistrates were told.

Eventually, in June 2003, he was convicted of drink-driving, banned for two years and fined £1,500. It transpired that he had drunk an entire bottle of wine before driving the short distance to pay his newspaper bill.

After eventually getting his licence back, Nigel's driving became life threatening. But it had nothing to do with drink. His friend Michael Corry-Reid recalls, 'Nigel was telling the same stories twice, without noticing. And his driving was frightening. He kept scraping the kerb.' He was ultimately diagnosed with PSP. In its later stages, Nigel lost the power to see, speak, move or swallow. Before total paralysis, Nigel had been secreting his medication in the hope of being able to end it all with an overdose rather than endure the hell on earth of the final stages of the disease. He was unable to carry out his own wish and died, aged sixty-five, in July 2007.

At his funeral, the priest declared that Dempster might have to spend a million years in purgatory, pausing just long enough to shock the congregation before adding that, in eternity, a million years would pass in the snap of a finger.

But, for the Proctor family, there was one final indignity before his death. They received a bill for £400 for the damage caused to Nigel's car by the coke bottle Kylie's sister had flung at it as Nigel sped away.

Kylie says, 'I got a few thousand pounds' compensation, which really didn't make up for the damage to my leg. I didn't know Nigel and wasn't aware he had died. I have no bitterness. It is just one of those things that happen in life.'

Nigel's illness was in its early stages when he offered me a job as his deputy in 1998. The previous incumbent, Adam Helliker, had departed after a fist fight with Nigel, which resulted in Adam's lower lip resembling that of the flesh saucepan possessed by the rain forest inhabitant Sting used to parade about on TV chat shows.

At the time I was still William Hickey, but the new editor Rosie Boycott didn't see the point of the column. She had recently replaced Richard Addis and was baffled by the cast of eighteenth-century characters I had incorporated to compliment Hickey – a real-life eighteenth-century Irish diarist.

One of Rosie's first acts was to summon me to her office and announce the killing off of Munnoo. This was Hickey's real-life manservant, reincarnated in Henry Fitzherbert, my brilliant deputy. The device was that Hickey failed to understand modern life, baffled by celebrity, mobile telephones, television and modern music.

Henry, alias Munnoo, attended parties and had his finger on the pulse of hip London. He knew about the internet, had a mobile telephone and was aware of who was who in *Coronation Street*, *Emmerdale* and the rest of the TV soaps.

He was complemented by a manservant called Roberts (a salute to previous Hickey regular John Roberts), an oily under butler called Nigel (a poke at Dempster), a glamorous assistant, Charlotte (in real life Charlotte Edwards) and a dog called Caesar. Apart from Roberts and Nigel, the cast of characters actually did exist in the time of Hickey. Jilly Cooper even offered to find us a dog called Caesar and look after him for the Diary.

'Get rid of Munnoo,' ordered Rosie. Tongue in cheek, I explained that it would cost a fortune in redundancy. 'He's been with Hickey since 1780,' I ventured. Rosie was unamused.

My top team also included Kathryn Spencer, Julie Carpenter and Kate Bogdanovich, supplemented by a rotating cast of journalist students from the University of Missouri. While bright, they knew little of British life, one asking, 'How can I join the royal family?'

Another I asked to call the late Lord Blake, the historian of the Conservative Party, to check if Woodrow Wyatt's allegation in his newly published diary that Harold Macmillan had been buggered at Eton was true. The intern asked, 'What is buggery?' When I explained, he said, 'Oh, in Missouri we call that butt-fucking.'

One of my top casuals was James O'Brien, now a star of LBC and BBC *Newsnight*. He worked selling suits in Aquascutum in Regent's Street and provided regular tips on celebrity customers, including John Major.

One day I noticed that Henry Fitzherbert and other members of the Hickey team were kitted out in expensive suits from Aquascutum. I made enquiries and discovered that James was entitled to buy a number of £500 suits from Aquascutum for family and friends at half price and Fitzherbert and other members of the team were recipients of this bargain.

'What about the boss?' I bleated. Shamefacedly, James explained that he had exceeded his allocation for that year. Then he had a brain wave. Why didn't he tell his boss that he was giving his dad a surprise Aquascutum suit for Christmas and a friend who had the same measurements as Mr O'Brien Sr would be coming in to the shop the following Saturday morning to be measured for the gift? I was to be that friend. Perfect!

The following Saturday I was bringing my youngest son Jack, then aged five, to a Rupert Bear party at Planet Hollywood. Afterwards I took his hand and he accompanied me the short walk to Aquascutum in Regent's Street. As soon as I asked to be directed to James on the first floor I knew there was something amiss.

Extras from *Are You Being Served?*, tape measures draped around their necks, looked at me with contempt. An agitated James, also equipped with said measure, grabbed me and took me to a corner of the store. With indecent haste he selected the jacket of a double-breasted blue pinstripe suit from a rack. 'Put this on,' he hissed. I took the trousers and found a changing room. When I emerged, James dramatically swished a piece of chalk over the shoulders, armpits and crotch. I removed the suit and came back to James clutching my wallet. 'How much do I owe you?' I asked. James had a look of horror on his face. His eyes darting over my shoulder at the glaring staff, he said, 'Don't give me any money. Can you go? NOW?' I departed with Jack.

It transpired that, earlier that morning, after James had explained his plan to his manager, his father had

unexpectedly paid a visit to the suit emporium to say
hello to his son. Now the late Mr O'Brien was not quite
as small as Ronnie Corbett, but he was not by any measure remotely near my 6 ft 2 in. height. The game was up
for James at Aquascutum ... but not before I was delivered of a splendid double-breasted pinstripe suit for a
mere £50 – James had miraculously found an invisible
flaw in the pinstripe that reduced the price of the suit to
the level of Primark's finest.

It was as William Hickey that we devised the National
Treasure lunches to coax celebrities to the sixth-floor
boardroom of the *Express* for a splendid nosebag, where
they could be relieved of gossip and tittle-tattle for the
column. We are talking 1996, before the term 'National
Treasure' was totally devalued.

Each week I commissioned the *Express* cartoonist
Griffin to draw a caricature of a treasure and we would
run this with a tongue-in-cheek eulogy in my Saturday
page. I picked recipients who deserved the NT description and included Sir John Mortimer, Dame Barbara
Cartland, Cardinal Hume and Bill Deedes.

Our inaugural get-together was a triumph. I was astonished at the stature of personalities who accepted our
invitations (we did send cars to their homes to collect and
ferry them back). I sat at the top end of the coffin-shaped

table flanked by my hero Sir Terry Wogan and the adorable Jilly Cooper. Guests at that first nosebag included Lord and Lady Longford, Quentin Crewe, Auberon Waugh, Lew Grade and the nearly blind Sir John Mills, who peered at me during the welcoming speech through a brass telescope. He sat next to Dame Barbara Cartland, who flirted with him throughout the lunch.

My young deputy Henry Fitzherbert sat beside his hero Lord Grade and at the pudding stage accepted a jumbo Monte Cristo cigar from the TV and movie mogul. It was pre-smoking ban and Grade and Fitzherbert puffed away to their hearts' content.

Sir Terry, assuming that the Havanas had been provided by *Express* owner Lord Stevens, nudged me and asked if he too might have a cigar.

I summoned a waiter and asked if the proprietor's cigar box, located in his private dining room nearby, might be relieved of a cigar for my guest Sir Terence Wogan. The waiter nodded, left the room and returned with a Delph saucer. On it was a single Hamlet, a poor excuse for a stogy. Terry, glancing at young Fitzherbert, his head thrown back and curls of delicious Cuban smoke swirling about him, was disappointed.

The lunches continued at three-monthly intervals with a high calibre of guests – Sir Cameron Mackintosh,

George Melly, Thora Hird, Anna Ford, Johnny Morris, Patrick Moore, June Whitfield, George Alagiah and Peter Stringfellow, to name a few.

Spike Milligan was in one of his good moods when he travelled up from his home in Rye for one of our lunches. Though frail and within two years of death, he enjoyed himself immensely. At a subsequent Irish embassy reception, Spike was noticeable as the only guest sitting in a chair during the ambassador's speech. I had a spare invitation in my pocket for our next National Treasure lunch and quickly wrote Spike's name on it, walked across the room and handed him the envelope. He quickly placed it in the inside pocket of his blue blazer. Then, as I watched, he retrieved the envelope, put on his glasses and read the contents. He removed the glasses, peered around the ballroom, spotted me and laboriously rose to his feet and slowly shuffled towards me, holding the invitation and torn envelope in his hand. 'Couldn't you afford a fucking stamp?' he asked and turned on his heels.

I took that as a refusal. Then, due to lack of celebrities, the lunch was cancelled and the few acceptances were informed. We forgot about Spike. On the particular day, I received a telephone call to say that Spike Milligan was in reception for lunch. No one had informed him that the event was not taking place. Spike, not in the best of health, had made his own way up from Rye for our National Treasures lunch!

Poignantly, exactly a month later – it happened to be a Friday, when no one worked on the Diary – I received a call at home from reception at the *Daily Express* in Blackfriars. It was Spike again. He had clearly misread his diary and made another fruitless journey from Rye.

While I prospered under the editorship of Richard Addis, he was astonishingly craven when it came to offending his friends. Once I asked Hickey diarist Charlotte Edwards to call then *Sunday Telegraph* editor Dominic Lawson to confirm a story I'd heard. It concerned a curious request from Diana, Princess of Wales, to her friend Rosa Monckton, Dominic's wife and then boss of a posh Bond Street jewellery company. Rosa had recently suffered a miscarriage. Diana asked if she and Dominic would allow the baby's body to be buried in her private garden at Kensington Palace. The couple agreed and the tragic mite was discreetly interred.

Charlotte called Dominic and asked, 'Was the story true?' Lawson was apoplectic with fury at the audacity of Charlotte. He declined to say anything. Within the hour, I was summoned to the editor's office. Dominic had called Richard to complain. Addis immediately took the side of the furious Lawson. 'I want you to sack

Charlotte.' I pointed out she was freelance. 'Well, don't ever use her again,' countered Richard.

'I was the one who asked her to call Dominic,' I said. 'If anyone is to be sacked, it is I.' I didn't expect to be fired and wasn't. Charlotte continued to work for me and went on to a stellar career as a star interviewer. She was responsible for another bizarre royal story.

She mentioned that her dad, a senior figure in the Royal Navy, had been the examiner when Prince Andrew sat his naval exams. When she mentioned this, her father was then in charge of a NATO base in Portugal. He retained a copy of the Duke of York's answers to the examination questions. I mumbled half-heartedly that it would be interesting to see the results.

A week later, Charlotte returned from a weekend with her parents in Portugal and pointed theatrically to a large buff envelope on my desk, addressed to William Hickey. I opened it. It contained a copy of Andrew's handwritten answers.

Charlotte had found the file and, without her dad's knowledge, copied the document on his fax machine. When I explained that if I used the material it would probably ruin her father's Royal Navy career, Charlotte replied, sweetly, 'But Daddy will never know. The *Express* isn't on sale in Portugal.' She was very young.

Richard had a delightfully eccentric secretary called Stella, who worked the late shift in Ludgate House. A sweet-faced girl and a Buddhist, she was a charmingly chubby figure with enormous breasts that swayed alarmingly as she trotted about the editorial floor. After Richard was fired and replaced by Rosie Boycott, she was devastated. I took her to the nearby Stamford's wine bar across the street for a consoling drink.

'Poor Richard,' she wailed. 'He was under such pressure. I did what I could to help him. In the evenings he often asked me into his office when there was no one about, told me to shut the door and asked me to dance and jump about the office. He just sat behind his desk watching me.'

After Richard was unexpectedly sacked by Lord Hollick, I cannily sought out the friends of former Spare Rib founder Rosie and went about ingratiating myself. Australian firecracker Kathy Lette, wife of liberal lawyer Geoffrey Robertson, was hugely helpful, but I had a bit less luck with Rosie's best mate Sally O'Sullivan. Her ex-husband Charlie Wilson, formerly editor of *The Times*, pointed her out at a drinks party in the library of the Reform Club on Pall Mall and suggested I should introduce myself to her.

Glass of claret in hand, I sauntered over and cheekily

asked her to 'talk me up' with Rosie. Her eyes blazed: 'Certainly not,' she snapped. 'I've never set eyes on you before in my life.' I could hear, and feel, the trickle of claret onto my shoes from my tilted glass.

Six months after Rosie took over, Dempster offered me a job. The salary was only £10,000 more than the £60,000 I was then earning but I was of a mind to take it. I agreed in principle after a drink in the Royal Garden Hotel Kensington with the *Mail*'s editor Paul Dacre. The following evening I had a pint of foaming ale with Chris Blackhurst, the deputy editor of the *Express* near Waterloo. I confided my decision, greatly inflating the salary offer, as journalists do.

Chris promised to speak to Rosie. The next day, I was summoned to her office. 'I want you to stay,' she said. 'I'll give you £100,000 a year and change the name of the column from Hickey to McEntee.' I was pleasantly stunned. We shook hands on it. I biked a letter to Paul Dacre immediately explaining the reason for not accepting his offer.

Others weren't so lucky with Rosie. She sacked a lot of people; none of them had the pleasure of a face-to-face meeting. Managing editor Lindsay Cook was Madame Guillotine, summoning people to break the bad news and then offering them terms. One, Tom McGee, the City editor, said he had a young family. She winked and suggested that he could be generous in filling in his last expenses claim. Another, James Hughes-Onslow, said he had a son starting at Eton. Miss Cook asked how he could afford to send a son to Eton on his salary. Hughes-Onslow Jr was a scholarship boy. Shortly after his sacking, James exacted revenge.

Commissioned by James Steen, editor of *Punch*, to view Rosie's house in Westbourne Grove, which was then on the market, he did more than Steen had asked. The estate agent arranged a viewing, not knowing James was a disgruntled ex-employee.

In the coming weeks, Rosie and her family were troubled by a noxious smell emanating from the bathroom. It grew in potency and eventually a plumber was summoned. He could find nothing wrong with the drains. Finally, in a recess behind the bath panel, he discovered a packet of rotting fish fingers. Rosie was incandescent. She got her secretary Tamsin to painstakingly telephone each of the potential vendors who had viewed the property. She hit the jackpot when James – who had used his wife's maiden name with the agents – answered his telephone brightly: 'James Hughes-Onslow here.' Rosie threatened to prosecute for criminal trespass but the story was allowed to slip quietly into Fleet Street folklore.

James was a deceptively colourful character. Quiet and unprepossessing, royal Principal Private Secretary Michael Peat had been his fag at Eton. He was also friendly with Tony and Cherie Blair and wrote the biography of John Major's Pooterish brother Terry Major-Ball.

While a junior reporter on the *London Evening Standard*, he was sent to cover the first Notting Hill Carnival. A riot ensued and James took shelter in a doorway. The door was opened by the occupant, Germaine Greer, author of *The Female Eunuch*. This was in the '70s and Germaine was a stunning-looking woman with a ravenous sexual appetite. *Standard* myth says James was gone for weeks, but he did have a prolonged fling with Greer. As a bachelor about town at the time, why not?

Before Rosie sacked James, I had been invited by Fiona Duff, the lovely publicist who famously chronicled her divorce from *Have I Got News* creator Harry Thompson in the *Daily Mail* (he had bolted with Victoria Coren), to a recording of the BBC TV programme *Room 101*, with Germaine Greer.

It was filmed at the South Bank TV Centre, a short stroll from the HQ of the *Express* on Blackfriars Road. After the recording, Fiona, Germaine and I joined the producer for a glass of wine.

'I work with an old friend of yours,' I ventured to Germaine, explaining that it was James Hughes-Onslow. I expected her to exclaim, 'Who?' Quite the contrary. Moving a step closer and fixing me firmly with her eyes. 'Dear James. How is he?' she asked. I told her that James was currently employed writing the Beachcomber column. 'Do you know,' declared Germaine in a matter-of-fact, everyday voice, 'James has the biggest cock of any man I have ever slept with.'

To say I was flabbergasted would be an understatement. I can normally talk for Ireland with the rest of Europe thrown in. I was, however, rendered speechless upon hearing this pronouncement. I never told James this tale but recently I found myself attending an *Oldie* lunch in Simpson's-in-the-Strand. Rosie was sat next to me and James, who writes the magazine's memorial services, was at an adjoining table. Mischievously, I asked Rosie if she'd forgiven him for what had gone into Fleet Street lore as the 'Fish Finger Incident'.

'No,' she replied. 'I think he is a shit.' Still in pursuit of mischief, I told her the Germaine Greer story. Her reaction was both curious and revealing.

As I finished on Greer's quote about James's enormous cock, Rosie piped up, 'Not as big as Anthony Haden-Guest's…' No, I didn't ask.

During Rosie's editorship she took the build-up to the 2000 millennium very seriously indeed. She installed a special clock atop the building overlooking the Thames, which offered pedestrians a countdown to the new century through 1999.

I had taxied from home to the office on the evening of 31 December 1999 to join Rosie and other members of staff preparing the last twentieth-century edition of the *Express*. Most of us – not Rosie – had refreshed ourselves earlier in the Young's pub the Mad Hatter just across Blackfriars Bridge Road from the office.

Rosie naturally wanted to mark the end of one millennium and the beginning of another with a striking front page. As midnight approached, dozens of people swarmed back to the office from the nearby pub to enjoy a strategic view of Bob Geldof's fireworks on the Thames, flowing majestically alongside the *Express* HQ.

Rosie was poring over a selection of photographs, trying to decide what should grace the front page of the first *Express* of the new century. Should she go with the Queen lighting the first beacon, the celebrity antics at the infamous Dome or the fireworks exploding overhead?

On the horns of a dilemma, she was delighted when a young chap standing alongside her emphatically pointed at a particular snap and said, 'That's the one. Go with it.'

Rosie took his advice, selected the shot and then came over to the window to join her senior colleagues for a New Year's toast. Pointing to the young tyro who had helped her make her historic decision, she asked her deputy Chris Blackhurst, 'Who is that over there? He is very good.' Blackhurst peered at the talented young operative and confessed he hadn't a clue. It was No. 3 Chris Williams who solved the problem. 'Oh, he's the barman from the Mad Hatter pub across the road. He just followed us over...'

Like everyone else, Rosie was stunned when Lord Hollick sold the *Express* to Richard Desmond for £125 million in 2000. Desmond, millionaire publisher of *OK!* magazine and a stable of porn titles including *Asian Babes*, was not considered a suitable newspaper proprietor.

Perhaps remorseful of his decision to sell to Desmond, Labour peer Hollick sent extraordinarily generous gifts of £40k to certain members of staff, including me. (Unfortunately, I'd just left my wife. She got the cheque and I was lumbered with the £12,000 tax bill for the windfall.)

The list was not based on seniority or longevity or

even worth. I had met Lord Hollick twice at the theatre. His largesse caused great dissent at the *Express*, with those unjustifiably ignored resentful of those who had received the money.

Rosie apparently went to Hollick with a list of names she felt should have been included.

Clive Hollick patiently explained that he had divided a £1 million pie into £40,000 segments. He could not add any more names without removing some of the recipients.

Fleet Street myth suggests Rosie returned with another list – this time of people who should be deleted. I don't believe it but if she did it was too late to change the proprietor's plan. (I hope my name wasn't on that second list, Rosie!)

But it was Rosie's reaction to the Desmond takeover that was most damaging. Awaiting a financial agreement on the terms of her departure, she stubbornly refused to engage with Desmond. He would arrive on the newsroom floor each evening, accompanied by his bearded Rasputin, smoking a Monte Cristo cigar. Rosie was nowhere to be seen.

Rosie kept out of Desmond's way at that year's *Express* Christmas party, too, held at the nearby Mermaid Theatre on the north bank of the Thames. At the time, John

Diamond was the paper's star columnist. It was John's last Christmas. He was dying of throat cancer but bravely continued working right up to the end. Married to Nigella Lawson, John had suffered the indignity of having his tongue removed as part of his draconian treatment. He was thus rendered mute. Wherever he went, he brought a small notepad and pen and feverishly scribbled responses to questions and enthusiastically joined in any conversation.

John and I were thus chatting when Richard Desmond loomed into view. I introduced him to John. Desmond seemed baffled with the confetti-like notes John handed him as he asked him about his work for the *Express*. As his voice rose louder I could only assume that he thought John was deaf as well as mute.

Then he glanced at Diamond's final note and abruptly departed our company. I asked John what he'd written. He re-scribbled the note and, with a lopsided grin, showed it to me. It read: 'Fuck Off'.

Less than three months later, I was at John's funeral at Kensal Crematorium. As I viewed the wreaths after the ceremony, Ruby Wax, in leggings and a scarlet jacket, ran from the chapel and scrunched to her knees on the crematorium gravel path. 'Why John, God!? Why!?' she screeched, waving her mitts at the sky. I was standing close to actor Alan Rickman, who had accompanied Ruby to the funeral. I remarked that she was very upset. Out of the side of his mouth the *Truly, Madly, Deeply* star lisped, 'I think she met him twice.'

Back at the *Express*, the sandwiches accompanying her roadmap sufficiently filled, Rosie finally departed and was replaced with Chris Williams.

It was only after Rosie had packed her pyjamas for pastures new that I heard of her antics when secretly negotiating with Harrods owner Mohamed Al-Fayed to purchase the *Express* from Lord Hollick. This was clearly before Desmond got his grubby hands on the paper.

After one lunch at Harrods in Knightsbridge with Mohamed, accompanied by her roly-poly deputy Christ Blackhurst, the Egyptian tycoon made an attractive offer. 'Rosie, you want fur coat?' Rosie's affirmative nod was as enthusiastic as a youngster accepting an offer to tour Disneyland without queuing.

Mo turned to Blackhurst: 'Baldie, you want fur coat for wife?' Blackhurst, who was indeed as bald as a billiard ball, declined the offer. But he did accompany the proprietor and his editor to the lift and descended into the bowels of the Knightsbridge emporium. They fetched up in a humidified room filled with racks of perfectly preserved fur coats.

Blackhurst correctly reckoned that the coats had been left in storage by Dowager Duchesses and the like, inhabitants of the nearby posh boulevards of Hans Crescent and Eaton Square. They had expired without their families realising where the fur coats were stored.

Rosie tried on a mink and then blatantly asked for a second coat for her daughter Daisy. She left, arms laden with the two furs. Weeks later she was distressed when her company car was broken into during a visit to her aged dad in Ludlow. Nothing was taken except for the pair of fur coats stolen from the boot of the car. Mo no longer owns Harrods, but is it possible Rosie's coats have resumed their perches in a temperature-controlled rack in the basement of the store? We will never know.

My own encounter with Mohamed was less lucrative but nonetheless bizarre. After Phil Hall was fired as editor of the *News of the World* in 2000, he became Mohamed's media adviser. This was bad news for James Steen, editor of Al-Fayed's magazine *Punch*. He had turned Hall into an enemy with a scurrilous piece of gossip in his media column Reptile House.

As part of Hall's anti-Steen strategy, I was invited to have lunch with Mohamed.

It took some time for me to realise that I was being sounded out as a possible editor of *Punch*.

Lunch was surreal. Beforehand, I sat in a sofa in a wood-panelled waiting room outside Mo's office. He arrived in shirtsleeves, the familiar striped silk shirt with a white collar.

'I bring you gift from Harrods,' he said, depositing a large, familiar green shopping bag on my lap. 'It is a gold bar,' he added. Inside was a giant, gold chocolate bar confection from Terry's. It was accompanied by two Turnbull & Asser silk ties. They were clip-ons and curiously short.

Mohamed towered over me as I examined my gifts. 'Look,' he declared, whipping off his own clip-on neckwear. 'You wear these ties, you never get strangled.'

Then, dramatically, he ripped open his shirt to expose a white round-neck vest. I was expecting to see a Superman-like logo declaring WonderMo.

'See,' he explained. 'Velcro buttons.' Then, fingering the zip on his fly, he asked, 'You want to see my cock?' I declined.

Flanked by two security guards whispering into their cuffs like extras in a Hollywood movie about the President of the United States, I walked the short journey down the corridor with Mo to the Green Room restaurant. The menu of melon and salmon was not negotiable. Neither was the bread-and-butter pudding. What Mo ate, we ate.

Mo did not trouble the bottle of Chablis on the table until the dessert arrived. Curiously, he poured spoonfuls of the wine onto the pudding, creating an ice cream sundae-type mess.

The conversation was dominated by references to the penis size of a variety of well-known people and members of the royal family. He did weep once, after getting agitated and accusing 'the fuggin' Duke of Edinburgh' of conspiring to have his son Dodi killed in Paris with the Princess of Wales.

Throughout the meal, the Harrods chairman was flanked by bodyguards standing at each shoulder. Why they were not obliged to actually taste his food I know not.

Needless to say, nothing came of my *Punch* editorship and the magazine discreetly vanished from the newsstands. Mohamed never got his fuggin' British citizenship.

When Al-Fayed revived *Punch*, he hired my friend Peter McKay to edit it.

Peter had ambitions to make *Punch* the British equivalent of the *New Yorker*. But Peter was more talented as a writer than an editor. His deputy, Mike Molloy, complained about his lack of decision-making, saying he had to chase Peter around the office with the equivalent of a butterfly net to get him to make up his mind about the forthcoming edition.

Peter was soon back in the *Daily Mail* fold and my friend James Steen made a decent fist of turning *Punch* into a sophisticated *Private Eye*. His sworn enemy, Phil Hall, former editor of the *News of the World*, tired himself out trying to blame Mohamed's failure to secure a coveted British passport on Steen's incurable irreverence.

Before all that, however, when Peter began his tenure at *Punch*, he immediately commissioned all his chums to write for the magazine. One of them was Keith Waterhouse, the brilliant playwright and columnist for the *Daily Mirror* and then the *Daily Mail*.

I still miss my friend and drinking companion Keith. We were neighbours in Earls Court when I started working for the *Daily Mail* in 2001. The curmudgeonly Keith spent much of his last decade in O'Neill's, a giant barn of a pub on the corner of Earls Court and Brompton Road now called The Bolton.

The Leeds-born scribe, who was once famously mocked by journalistic colleague Paul Callan as specialising in nostalgic articles about old tram tickets, was famous for *Billy Liar* and *Jeffrey Bernard is Unwell*. When his lesser-known play *Hear My Song* was revived in Bath, with Peter Bowles starring, I organised a

NOT ONE TO GOSSIP, BUT...

train-carriage-load of chums to travel down for the opening night. 'How long does it take to get to Bath?' I asked Keith. 'A bottle and a half of Chardonnay,' he replied.

Keith's survival into his ninth decade – he died aged eighty-one in 2010 – was a medical wonder. He supplemented his meagre breakfast of fruit with a daily Niagara of Pinot Grigio consumed by the glass (never the bottle) at home and in O'Neill's.

To my cost, I discovered Keith's stubborn adherence to his 'just the one glass' philosophy (i.e. just the one glass *at a time*, that is).

When the pub launched a promotion offering the rest of the bottle when two large glasses were purchased, I returned to our table clutching the bottle. Keith glared at it before pointing an accusing finger: 'What is THAT?'

I explained. He was having none of it. As I attempted to replenish his half-empty glass he placed his hand over it. 'No, I don't want a bottle.' He then shuffled to the bar and ordered two large glasses of white wine. When the barman insisted on handing over the entire bottle, Keith objected. 'I don't want the rest of it, pour it down the sink.' He then turned in exasperation towards me and bellowed, 'We'll be here all day!'

On another occasion, returning from a trip to Venice, I enthused about the beauty of the Italian city. I was in mid-spout when Keith raised a hand and declared, 'Sorry, I don't do scenery.'

On another occasion I mentioned the late Spike Milligan. 'I never liked him,' offered Keith, before pausing to sip his wine and exclaim, 'In fact, I LOATHED him.'

But he did like the late media lawyer Oscar Beuselinck, scourge of newspapers on behalf of his clients. When his second marriage was on the rocks, he contacted Oscar. Keith recalled that he had said, 'So the cat has pissed on the strawberries again?' This recollection triggered a fit of the giggles.

He also enjoyed recalling his encounter with the late Robert Maxwell, who, on purchasing the *Mirror*, was keen to keep his star columnist on board (his subsequent defection to the *Mail* was engineered by the late Sir David English). Unaware that he was a freelancer, Maxwell summoned him and offered him a greatly enhanced *Mirror* pension if he would stay. Keith's reply: 'Mr Maxwell, I don't have a *Mirror* pension to enhance.'

Alas, our amiable imbibing was not without mishap. On one occasion Keith fell from his stool and knocked his head badly against a metal radiator. Fortunately he lived just across Old Brompton Road in

Coleherne Court and could be carried home without too much difficulty.

This, sadly, was a regular occurrence. But there were lighter moments. As the men's lavatory was above a sweeping staircase on the distant first floor, the management kindly provided Keith with a key to the disabled toilet on the ground floor. On one occasion, Keith engineered his half shuffle, half stagger from our table to the toilet past a group of youths clustered around the jukebox. By the time Keith emerged from the thunderbox, a rap record was playing loudly. As one Waterhouse shoe shuffled forward, tentatively followed by the other, his elbows wobbling to keep his balance, Keith made his slow progress back to his glass of Pinot Grigio. His berthing at the table coincided with the end of the record. The gaggle of youngsters, clearly impressed with Keith's dancing skills, gave him a round of applause.

Frequently I was obliged to carry the frail Worzel Gummidge figure the short distance from O'Neill's to his apartment at Coleherne Court. I always abided by the advice of the solicitous Irish housekeeper not to put Keith to bed, but to leave him on the floor. 'He won't fall out of bed that way,' he explained.

I've unearthed this extract from my diary, dated Thursday 31 March 2006:

Lunch at Langans Coq d'Or. John Edwards, Jeff Powell, Bill Hagerty and the Great Waterhouse. He shuffles in at 1.30 and complains ten minutes after sitting down that he can't reach the white wine marooned in an ice bucket just out of reach.

Three times he asks the Polish waitress to bring it to him and three times she misunderstands and merely tops up his already brimming glass. Eventually I call her aside and point at the bottle. She thinks I want some white wine. Edwards goes over, lifts the dripping bottle from its moorings and planks it down in front of Keith.

We order starters and main courses. Keith asks for an eggs Benedict starter. It is hardly substantial. By 4 p.m. Keith is slumped in his chair, most of two bottles residing in his tummy with the half-eaten eggs Benedict abandoned on the table. 'I must go to my beautiful home,' he declares and tries to rise. He slumps back in his seat. He tries again. He fails again. He is beached, stranded, incapable of traction. I go out to Old Brompton Road and hail a taxi explaining to the driver we have a distinguished if feeble writer who lives within sight of the restaurant who needs to get home. The driver is young and helpful. Hagerty and I manhandle Keith to the door of the cab and get him seated.

I accompany him the few hundred yards through the

traffic lights. The driver does a U-turn and parks outside Coleherne Court. Keith is now inert, asleep and incapable of independent movement. I try and lift him. No luck.

The driver comes round to the passenger door to help. I manoeuvre Keith so his feet are dangling out of the taxi. I am holding him under his arms. The driver lifts his feet but as I exit the cab Keith's jacket slips off and he lands gently on the pavement.

His blue shirt is now scrunched up around his neck, exposing his scrawny stomach. He remains comatose. The Irish housekeeper and his wife dash to our assistance. Together we get Keith through the door and onto a chair in the hall. I dash out and pay the taxi driver. After a short breather, the housekeeper and I carry Keith to the small lift to bring him to his flat on the second floor. Leaving Keith propped up against the housekeeper, I get into the elevator. The housekeeper pushes him into my bear hug and presses the button to the second floor. The housekeeper dashes up the stairs to greet the lift. We decant Keith and carry him to his front door. I fumble in his pocket for his keys, disturbing a sleeping wad of £300 in £20 notes.

I open the door and we drag Keith down the hallway to the bedroom on the left. I try lifting him onto the bed. The housekeeper tells me to desist. 'Lay him on the floor,' he instructs. I put a pillow behind his head and as I depart Keith raises an arm in salute. By the time I get back to the restaurant I am dishevelled. 'Thanks a lot, chaps,' I say. Cue laughter.

Friday 1 April: I call at 10 a.m. to see if Keith is OK. He picks up after the message. 'How are you?' I ask. 'I'm fine,' he replies. 'Just a little stiff after my sleep on the floor. See you soon.' Click.

Another extract:

25 February 2005:

I leave him at the door of O'Neill's. He resists my offer of an arm home. I watch as he shuffles unsteadily towards the traffic light on Old Brompton Road, Columbo raincoat flapping as he waits for green, his white mane of hair fluttering in the breeze, his forehead wearing a small Band-Aid placed on the cut he suffered two weeks ago when he crashed down in O'Neill's connecting horribly with the cast-iron radiator.

Two females drinking at the table chosen for Keith's collapse swung their wine glasses out of his trajectory as Keith toppled past them sliding down one side of the table onto the floor, his head coming to a halt against the cast-iron radiator. 'Am I bleeding?' he asked wanly. 'Yes,' I replied. I raised him to his feet, applying a tissue to the wound gushing scarlet. We proceeded on that occasion across traffic lights to Zafash the pharmacy. I had a mind to get some TCP and Elastoplast. The Indian proprietor comes rushing out saying, 'I am a doctor, come in.' Keith is brought in and placed in a chair where his wound is examined. It is a nasty cut and will swell up into a bump. The doctor sells me wipes and bandages, which Keith refuses to allow on his bonce. I link him home to Coleherne Court. We squeeze into the tiny lift up to the second floor along the corridor and safely berthed in his sitting room.

Opera plays on the radio, an empty bottle of Pinot Grigio stands on the hall table, another empty at his desk with the old Remington typewriter and a mound of papers. Surely he couldn't have polished two bottles before going out? Ex-wife and de facto carer Stella is away in Paris this weekend. I leave him propped on the sofa. A week later I conspire to leave him home by saying that I need to borrow his copy of H. G. Wells's *The Invisible Man.* He sees the subterfuge but after two bottles and a glass agrees that it is a good idea. We get home and safely ensconced he asks, 'Would you like the one?' I partake and then leave him.

12 March:

I am having a glass in O'Neill's when I see the familiar raincoat flapping about his knees clutching the traffic light standard outside Zafash as he waits for a light change to trundle across. I get him a drink. His former partner Willis Hall had died three weeks before, as had my old boss Ross Benson. Keith says, 'I divide the people I know between funerals and memorial services. Willis is a funeral, Ross is a memorial service.'

29 March:

Keith shuffles into O'Neill's unshaven, open-neck check shirt, sports jacket, fawn trousers. He asks what killed Ross Benson. I say it was a massive heart attack, adding that Keith had predicted his own death in a fall: 'Who told you that?' he snaps. I reply, 'You did.' He talks about his friend Peter O'Toole's drinking, saying, 'He's started again and more than before.' I remind him that we had asked O'Toole to join us at lunch in Langans. 'He won't make lunch because he is gone off to make a film in Spain or France or a country finishing with o,' says Keith. 'I can't see him doing *Jeffrey Bernard is Unwell* again … it was written for him and it's about my life not Jeffrey's. He has nothing to do with it. His daughter gets a percentage of the royalties, why I don't know, but it is. It is really Peter's play and I want him to do it again ... but it is so draining. Last time I saw him in the dressing room he had nothing left.' He talks a bit about Willis Hall. 'If we hadn't met I'd still have done *Billy Liar*. I'd still have done other things, only different.'

I'd asked him as a member of the Chelsea Arts Club if he'd write to the chairman endorsing my application to join. 'I'll do better than that,' he said. 'I'll have a drink with him and see what's occurring.' I ask him if he's made any progresses. 'Oh yes. I did have a drink and he said, and I quote, "We don't want his sort around here."' (My two applications were both rejected.)

Keith then goes off to the nearby disabled lavatory. He is shaky on his feet. After two bottles I fear for him. 'Can I leave you home?' I ask. 'No,' he replies. 'I want to read my paper.'

Inevitably he suffered the catastrophe we had all feared. After a subsequent lunch at Richard Shepherd's Langan's Coq d'Or with myself, Ian Wooldridge, Peter McKay and John Edwards, during which Keith merely frolicked with another portion of eggs Benedict washed down with copious quantities of Pinot, he was assisted home by John Edwards. Then seventy and in possession of a heart pacemaker, here is John's recollection of the journey.

I've said we went home by rail, that is, clutching the railings outside the apartments on Old Brompton Road. When we got to the traffic light at the end of Earls Court Road, I managed to get Keith halfway across when he slipped onto the tarmac. The lights went from red to green and cars were hooting their horns as I tried to lift Keith. They must have changed from green to red and back to green half a dozen times and I couldn't get him up. Eventually a pharmacist in Zafash, the all-night chemist shop on the corner, took pity on me and came over and lifted Keith and propped him up against the railings on Coleherne Court. I was able to manage the rest of the journey.

John made the fatal mistake of putting Keith to bed. At some stage in the night, he fell onto the floor, fracturing his right arm. He lay entangled in the lead from his bedside lamp for more than twelve hours. If his ex-wife Stella had not arrived some time the following morning, clutching a classic film on DVD to watch with Keith, he would have joined writing partner Willis Hall in the celestial green room that day.

Even recuperating at the Chelsea and Westminster Hospital he had lost none of his vim. Chuckling at his berth in the Marie Celeste ward, he pointed to a large wicker basket containing fruit sent by his editor Paul Dacre. 'Anyone want a banana?' he asked. Then, musing on the gift, he sighed, 'I suppose the basket will come in useful for holding pens.'

Afterwards, trips to O'Neill's became less frequent. Walking my pug Bertie one evening, I spied through the saloon bar window Keith drinking alone. Luckily, I had a carpet bag, which allowed me to smuggle Bertie into the no-dogs-allowed drink emporium. In the course of our conversation, Bertie popped his head out of the bag. Keith's reaction? He simply observed, 'A dog' and went on imbibing. Visiting him before Christmas in 2008, I found a Howard Hughes unshaven recluse still sipping Pinot Grigio.

I urged him to make 2009 the year he resumed his perambulations. His response? 'I don't do "out" any more.' Keith was a founder member of the Useless Information Society, an all-male gathering of journalists and actors who congregated over food and mostly drink in Soho to spout useless facts. Kenny the pianist from Jerry's Club in Dean Street was our beagle, i.e. he wore a silly Admiral Nelson-type hat, a cloak and brandished a staff. His role was to rise to his feet in the middle of proceedings and pronounce an item just uttered 'Useful', thus shaming the member who thought his reference to the speed of an elephant's fart was completely useless.

The inaugural dinner for the UIS was held at Peter Boizot's L'Epicure restaurant on Dean Street in Soho in 1998. Waterhouse turned up with an old-fashioned cassette player from his ex-wife Stella in order to record the bon mots of the assembled members.

Jazz aficionado and ex-*Daily Mirror* man David Bradbury objected to Waterhouse's recorder, accusing him of intellectual theft. Bradbury raised a point of order, so beloved of Keith in his quaint columns about the non-existent local council oop north. The recorder was withdrawn.

Larger-than-life character Noel Botham, ex-*National Enquirer* scribe, brilliant Elvis impersonator and husband of the charming Lesley, landlady of the French House pub, conspired with publisher John Blake to make money from the Useless Information Society.

In fairness, Noel did all the work on the first *Book of Useless Information* published by Blake. Our names were included on the front cover as co-authors and it went on to sell more than 50,000 copies, sufficient to merit a ninth edition.

Apart from Noel and John, no one saw any money from this enterprise. It took some years to discover that we were all entitled to about £3,000 each from the royalties.

Five years before his death, Keith finally abandoned his beloved Useless Information Society. Financially well off, he wasn't bothered by the lack of royalties from the handbooks. But he was keen that whatever money was sloshing around should go to charity.

The charity he had in mind was The Passage, a Roman Catholic shelter for the homeless near Westminster Cathedral. Fr Michael Seed, Cardinal Hume's former adviser on ecumenism, was a member of the Useless Information Society and was associated with the charity. Keith wanted Fr Michael to have the money for the shelter.

Fr Michael, a Franciscan monk who liked a drink, was a slight, bespectacled figure with a tonsure and an innocent face. He was a regular on the party circuit and befriended many *Who's Who* entrants, including the Duchess of Kent. He became close enough to politicians Ann Widdecombe and John Gummer to convert them to Roman Catholicism. The joke wasn't that they had been Poped, but had gone to Seed.

He almost converted the late Alan Clark, the Tory Defence Minister and famous diarist. There is still an element of confusion, with Fr Michael continuing to hint that Alan did experience a death-bed conversion, while his widow Jane is adamant that he didn't.

It seems that Clark was keen and asked Seed if he

would be reunited with his beloved dogs when he went to heaven. Fr Michael put his foot in it, explaining that as dogs did not possess souls, they would not be in Paradise to greet their master. That, apparently, was it for Alan.

Whatever the truth, it sparked a debate on animals and heaven, with some arguing, in letters to *The Spectator*, that as heaven was what you wished for, if you wanted Rover or Tibbles to be there, they would.

These theological musings, however, were far from anyone's mind when Fr Michael became the Useless Information Society's honorary chaplain. All he had to do was say grace, drink his own body weight in wine and come up with a segment of useless information.

At Keith's last UIS dinner, upstairs at the French House, Botham finally conceded the existence of substantial royalties. Debate raged about how they should be spent. Noel, co-founder of the society, proposed that the money be used for a day trip to New York, where the members could partake of lunch. (Botham subsequently did invite the members to Paris for lunch to celebrate his sixty-ninth birthday. Three of the members missed the Eurostar back to London.)

New York sounded appealing, but the majority of members present, including myself, opted for the cash to be given to Fr Michael for his shelter.

A show of hands was called for. Only Botham voted against the donation to charity. He then rose to his feet and insisted that, as he had written the society's constitution and rules, he was overruling the vote. 'We will go to New York for lunch,' he declared, to a cacophony of spoons banging on the table.

Waterhouse got up on his hind legs and, pointing a finger at Fr Michael, said, 'I don't care what happens to the rest of the money, but I want my share to go to Fr Seed.'

More cutlery banging accompanied by cheers. Seed whispered something in Botham's ear. With a grin, Noel rose and said, 'Fr Michael says that if Keith gives him his share, he will use it to come to New York for lunch with the rest of us.'

Waterhouse walked out, never to be seen there again. Fr Michael had a successful autobiography ghosted by Noel and published by John Blake. He was extremely close to Noel and his devoutly religious wife Lesley.

A decade before our Useless Information debacle, Lesley asked Fr Michael to conduct an exorcism in the basement of the French House. Thames Water excavations had caused a flood and subsequent repairs, according to the deeply superstitious Lesley, had released evil spirits in the cellar. She believed that photographs of valued customers that lined the walls of the bar had begun, inexplicably, falling down, followed by the unexpected demise of the subject.

I was invited to witness the banishment ceremony.

The exorcism had been planned for 3 p.m. on 11 September 2001. We were not to know at the time of scheduling that at that precise moment, 3,600 miles away, hundreds of men and women were dying in the Twin Towers atrocity. At the very moment when Fr Michael Seed was to begin the ancient rite of banishing the devil in a Soho basement, more than 100 poor souls had already jumped to their deaths from the highest floors of the burning North Tower of the World Trade Center.

And when he was to deliver the exhortation, 'From all evil, deliver us, O Lord, from the snares of the devil', dozens of stricken and trapped victims were still making mobile telephone calls to loved ones who could do absolutely nothing to save them.

The awesome evil of 9/11 exactly coincided with a genuine, well-meaning and quaint attempt to banish evil.

The appointed hour was 3 p.m. London time. In New York, it was 9 a.m. Fourteen minutes earlier, American Airlines Flight 11 had plunged into the ninety-fourth floor of the North Tower of the World Trade Center. It fatally severed the building with a fireball that killed hundreds and trapped still more on the fourteen floors above. A total of 1,355 people at or above the point of impact were trapped and died of smoke inhalation, fell or jumped from the tower to escape the smoke and flames, or were killed in the building's eventual collapse.

A further 107 people below the point of impact did not survive. We did not know then that hijackers had directed a third plane into the Pentagon and a fourth had crashed in Pennsylvania. In all, almost 3,000 souls had perished that bright September morning of 9/11.

Four minutes after we should have started praying, United Airlines Flight 175 hurtled explosively into the neighbouring South Tower. One stairwell remained intact, allowing eighteen people to escape from above the point of impact, but 630 people died in the South Tower. Casualties were significantly reduced by the decision of some occupants to start evacuating when the North Tower was struck.

We were not to know all of this appalling carnage and destruction as we enjoyed a pre-ritual glass of wine in the crowded ground-floor bar of the French. But Sky News had just switched to live pictures of the burning North Tower, suggesting that a commercial jetliner had accidentally crashed into the iconic trade centre.

We watched mesmerised as a technicolour fireball suddenly splattered the clear blue sky. The South Tower had been struck at 2.04 London time, dispelling all lingering doubts about accidents.

It was a full two hours later – when both towers had crumbled to dust – that we finally tore our eyes away from the awful images coming live from New York. Perhaps for the first time in this rather louche watering hole, a minute's silence was observed for the victims.

It was Fr Michael's decision to go ahead with the exorcism. Struck dumb from what we had just seen, we sombrely trudged down the narrow stairs. All our minds were filled with images we had yet to fully comprehend.

There were only four of us: landlady Lesley and her husband Noel, Fr Michael and myself. There was something extraordinarily chilling in the age-old words he incanted. We shivered, not so much from the presence of evil in this subterranean space below teeming London but at the monstrous malice we had just witnessed more than 3,000 miles away.

Men and women starting their day's work on a gloriously sun-lit autumnal morning, equipped with all the sophisticated machinery of our world, computers and mobile telephones, had been annihilated in front of our eyes. How could the holy men who had devised this formula for confronting the devil have ever imagined the sheer scale of the malignancy unleashed by his modern cohorts at the start of the twenty-first century?

Holy water sprinkled the floor and walls. The priest walked through the connecting chambers clutching his prayer book and intoning the litany.

'I adjure you, ancient serpent, by the judge of the living and the dead, by your Creator, by the Creator of the whole universe, by Him who has the power to consign you to hell, to depart forthwith in fear, along with your savage minions.'

And who can doubt that on that sunny day in Manhattan these savage minions of the devil were about their master's business.

Raising his voice, Fr Michael, nearing the end of his exorcism, declared, 'By your cross and passion, by your death and burial, by your holy resurrection, by your wondrous ascension, by the coming of the Holy Spirit, the Advocate, on the day of judgement, by the mysteries of the incarnation, passion, resurrection, and ascension of our Lord Jesus Christ, by the descent of the Holy Spirit, by the coming of our Lord for judgement, I command you, moreover, to obey me to the letter.'

And, slowly, making the sign of the cross, he concluded, 'Begone, then, in the name of the Father, and of the Son, and of the Holy Spirit.' But where was God on 9/11?

Afterwards we went upstairs to the packed bar. What followed was surreal. Lesley asked Fr Michael if she could have the remainder of his holy water. He decanted it from his hip flask-like container into an empty wine glass on the bar.

Someone assumed it was white spirit and downed the contents. Lesley was upset and asked Fr Michael if he could make some more. He asked her to bring a decanter and some salt and he would create more holy water. She did. He placed the decanter, the salt and his crucifix on the shelf in front of the open window letting light in from Dean Street. Beside him on a stool perched Jaci Stephen, slightly the worse for wear, having been next door at the Groucho Club for lunch with Keith Waterhouse.

Lifting the front of her tight-fitting jumper up to her neck, she declared invitingly, 'Who wants to see my new breasts?' A stampede of old roués queued to poke, tweak and peer at Jaci's newly enhanced chest. At her elbow, Fr Michael was blissfully unaware of the forensic perusal of her mammaries.

EPILOGUE

No one drinks any more. No one goes out any more. No one meets people any more. Modern practitioners with their Prêt a Manger salad lunches and their five-a-day infusions at their work stations, their forensic reading of *Hello!*, *OK!* and *Closer*, sit from dawn till dusk at their winking computer screens.

All the national newspaper newsrooms are now filled with Terracotta Armies of earnest young men and women rewriting magazine articles and churning out a grim mince of show business and celebrity stories about people they don't know and will never meet.

And as for drinking – it's now confined to the canteen. As a self-confessed old fogey, I mourn the revolutionary transformation of a once-colourful and quixotic profession. Gone for ever is the once-conventional career path of getting a foot in the door in a local newspaper as a teenager or a job as a poorly paid copy boy on a national title and working your way up.

My generation had the benefit of inching vertically on the career ladder, junior reporters moving on to a specialisation – political, medical, social services – or the still-glorious peaks of sports reporting.

Now there is no middle ground. A journalistic Grand Canyon has evolved, marking the gap between the legion of poorly paid youngsters barnacled to their computers and, on the other side of the crevasse, very well-paid star writers, columnists and pundits occupying the distant high-altitude peaks.

There are a few dinosaurs still clinging on in the middle; veteran news reporters and specialists. And for those at the scorched-earth side of the canyon, a university education and a course in journalism are de rigueur for employment on a national title. And with starting salaries diminished to the early £20,000s, it has become a calling dominated by those who have rich parents able to afford to subsidise London accommodation and other costs.

I am conscious of my dinosaur status. I still work, as a freelance, on the *Daily Mail* alongside my mentor Peter McKay, editor of the Ephraim Hardcastle gossip column. There are diverting compensations. As I write, in May 2016, my eldest child Laura has just given birth to Max Patrick John Gavin. He is my third grandchild. I imagine holding his 8lb 4oz innocent frame up to the morning light and celebrating life and survival. Echoing in my ears is the exhortation of my magnificent mother Judy, who entered heaven in July 2015: 'But, John, you still have your health.' Well, Judy, apart from drinking too much, eating rubbish, suffering from Type-2 diabetes, high blood pressure and a knackered ankle, you have a point.

But I have clambered back on the carousel, not going quite as fast and certainly not earning as much, but rising and falling nonetheless. It may only be in a circle, but what the heck. To plunder my dear friend Peter McKay's all-purpose payoff: 'Isn't life grand!'

INDEX

INDEX

INDEX